AT HOME IN MEXICO

CHARLES ALLEN SMART

NEW ENGLAND HOLIDAY (NOVEL) 1931 • THE BRASS CAN-
NON (NOVEL) 1933 • R.F.D. (ESSAYS) 1938 • ROSSCOMMON
(NOVEL) 1940 • WILD GEESE AND HOW TO CHASE THEM
(ESSAYS) 1941 • SASSAFRAS HILL (NOVEL) 1947 • THE GREEN
ADVENTURE (PLAY) 1954 • AT HOME IN MEXICO (ESSAYS)
1957

CHARLES ALLEN SMART

DRAWINGS BY LEONARD BROOKS

At Home in Mexico

DOUBLEDAY & COMPANY, INC., GARDEN CITY, NEW YORK, 1957

NOTE: In a slightly shorter form, and illustrated, Chapter 18, "Homage to Hermenegildo Bustos," was published by *Américas,* and the author is grateful to the editors of that magazine for permission to reprint.

Library of Congress Catalog Card Number 57-7829

TO LEONARD AND REVA BROOKS

CONTENTS

PREFACE

There is a rapidly increasing group of Americans who were retired involuntarily before they felt that they had done all the good work that they could do; and now, still somewhat to my surprise and annoyance as well as amusement, I find myself a member of this group. After nearly thirty years of fairly active work in publishing, teaching, farming, the navy, and teaching again, with some direction and continuity provided by the writing and publication of seven books, I found myself nearing my fiftieth birthday with no job or prospects of one if I wanted it, with no clear function or even identity, and with recurrent duodenal ulcers that were the clear and humiliating result of my anxiety about this situation. However, "His eye is on the sparrow," and my wife and I found that we could rent our country home in Ohio to excellent tenants for enough money, with a favorable exchange rate, to live well here in an ancient town in central Mexico. Including visits to the United States from a few hours to a few months in length, we have now lived here four years, and this little book

is an attempt to distill and communicate some of the quality
of our life here. It records an attempt to remain alive, if not
quite in inaction, then without a function; and if it were not
a bit esoteric and pretentious, an alternative title might be:
Tao in Mexico. Almost any reader will be in a better position
than the writer to judge the success or failure of this attempt.
The actual title was suggested by that of Cynthia Bowles'
charming book, *At Home in India,* and I am thus indebted
and grateful to Miss Bowles.

In publishing a book of this intimate nature, I am naturally
fearful of violating the privacy of friends and others mentioned
in it, and of the town itself, already sufficiently invaded by
aliens. However, under any other name our town of San
Miguel de Allende, Guanajuato, would be as easy to identify
as Concord, Massachusetts, and the individual persons could
easily be found also. All I can trust is that the good will with
which I hope they are viewed will mitigate this violation of
their privacy and make it more humorous than offensive or
burdensome. After all, in its four hundred years of history
this town has survived with serenity worse violations than
any small book, the Mexicans are concerned with more basic
matters, and the Americans can learn from them.

Considering the very small but definite possibility that this
book may become popular, and that my enthusiasm for this
town and for life in it may infect other Americans variously
unprepared for them, I should like to point out here that,
although we live well on relatively few dollars, the life is not
as cheap as many newspaper and magazine articles have
claimed; that the altitude is not good for many heart condi-
tions, and jaundice, dysenteries, and other diseases are common; that the supplies of water and electricity are irregular
and disorganized; that the foodstuffs are in general poor in
quality; that the Spanish language and the Mexican character
are not so easy to learn as they are often supposed to be;
that the secondary schools do not provide good preparation
for American colleges; that the hospital is very poor by

American standards; that one must adjust himself mentally
and emotionally to widespread and severe poverty, illiteracy,
and ignorance; that the Roman Catholic Church has in
Mexico a unique position and quality, not to be quickly
judged; that as aliens, we, like Mexicans and other foreigners
in the United States, are wrapped up in red tape and sometimes subjected to illegalities and even to violence; and, in
short, that living in Mexico requires of us Americans some
health, gusto, and detachment. It is also good to feel the
individual human beings within the races and nations, and
the imminence of death. With some such attitude I suppose
we can feel at home almost anywhere.

AT HOME IN MEXICO

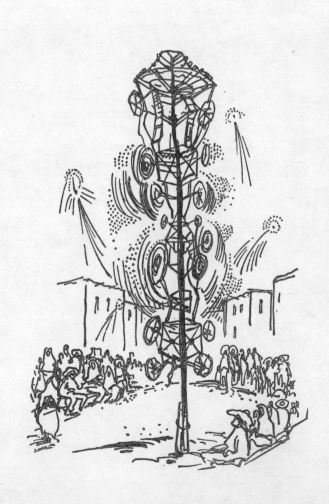

1. FACES IN THE FIRELIGHT

In what seemed to be the middle of the first night that we spent in San Miguel, during a shorter stay eight years ago, my wife Peggy and I were awakened by what sounded at first like gunfire, followed by the ringing of bells.

"This does it," I said. "We have traveled twenty-four hundred miles in search of an ivory tower and we have arrived in the middle of a revolution. Somebody is trying to take over the City Hall and the loyalists are ringing all the bells as an alarm."

It was four o'clock in the morning. When I put on a bathrobe and slippers and went out into the garden I could see rockets exploding over the town, and it was now clear that we were hearing firecrackers, not tommy guns. So! Some kind of a celebration. But what an odd time to begin one, well before dawn. Perhaps the Soviet Government had disintegrated suddenly in an explosion of derisive laughter. Perhaps there had been discovered simultaneously the causes and cures of cancer, polio, heart failure, the common cold, and demagoguery. Nothing less would justify such celebration.

It was not until morning that we learned that this was the fiesta of Corpus Christi, and that all of the regular feast days of the Church, plus a generous number of saints' days, were liberally celebrated in San Miguel. In fact, hardly a month passes here without some fiesta beginning thus at four in the morning and lasting at least into the following night and perhaps through several days and nights thereafter.

When we lived hard by the Parroquia, or leading parish church, these early morning fireworks and bells, sometimes accompanied by the town band, were often so loud that we could do nothing but dress, sally forth into the streets to see

the fireworks, and then join the shawled and hatted figures
hurrying in to Mass. Sometimes this early Mass is the end
of it until more celebrations that evening, but sometimes
the fireworks, bells, and band continue all day, along with a
little man who plays a fife and drum at the same time. He
manages to do this by holding and fingering the fife with his
left hand, hanging a small drum (decorated with landscapes)
from his left arm, and beating on the drum with his right
hand. What is more remarkable is the length of his performance. Recently, standing at the door of the chapel of Santo
Domingo, about seventy yards from our present house, with
only a few hours out for rest, he played two days and much
of the night between. We wondered whether his religious
devotion was assisted by marijuana.

In the ordinary little fiesta the celebration consists besides
extra Masses, of a parish or town gathering in the streets
outside of the church in question. Everyone stands around in
the street or sits on curbstones or in doorways. By everyone I
mean just that, from local gentry and tourists to large families
who have come in from the ranches with children, babies,
burros, food, cooking utensils, and mats and blankets for
sleeping on the sidewalks. Besides the fires for private meals,
there are those of the ever-present vendors of hot *tacos*,
peanuts, sweets, and drinks, so that impassive Indian faces
and figures of the young and old are picked out by the
flickering lights.

There may be an improvised *carcel*, or jail, to which unwary
men are hauled off by laughing girls and fined. Occasionally
a bull made of bamboo and paper, and spouting fireworks,
is rushed here and there through the crowd while everyone
dodges, shrieks, and laughs aloud. Sometimes a man will
wander about, very casually shooting off rockets or fire wheels
that often run amuck in the crowd and sometimes put out
people's eyes. A couple of years ago the gay and charming
lad who fetched our ice lost an eye in this manner, and the
other one was saved only because Señora Alemán, the wife

of the last President, had established an eye, ear, nose, and throat clinic in the neighboring city of Celaya. Miguel Alemán seems to have stolen huge sums of money from the taxpayers, but he also created many things of great use to the people.

The big and final event of a fiesta is the setting off of the *castillo*, or castle. This is an elaborate structure of poles and bamboo, twenty or thirty feet high, that is set up firmly in the street in front of the church by removing a few cobblestones and digging holes for the supporting poles of wood. Up the sides of this structure there are tiers of wheels and other moving parts, all made of bamboo, filled with gunpowder, and somehow connected together with fuses. When the first fuse has been lighted, one wheel will suddenly rotate, spurting colored fires and whistling, then the others in that tier will catch on, another tier will go off, then another, and finally, at the end, the whole structure is in motion and ablaze while hundreds of dark faces, lighted from within as well, stare up at this creation of wonder and delight. We must have seen more than a hundred *castillos* ourselves, but we still find it hard to resist going to see another, and the Mexicans, who have seen thousands of them, have to be near death to stay at home.

There are other kinds of fireworks too, such as fire balloons, jets that run back and forth on wires, and even simulated naval and air battles. One of the best we have ever seen was a curtain of fire, changing color every few minutes, that was hung from the shell-shaped façade of the little church of the Salud, near the market. The most elaborate are those of the great fiesta of San Miguel, which lasts for three or four days towards the end of September, and which begins at four in the morning, usually bitter-cold. The town is almost totally fireproof, and full advantage is taken of the fact. The façade of the Parroquia is a neo-Gothic filagree of pink stone, and when every aperture is alive with colored fires and smoke, while every bell is ringing until the air seems to shake, "Señor San Miguel Arcángel" must be highly pleased.

2.   A SMALL, WAILING CRY

At four o'clock one morning in August we were awakened by something more compelling than rockets.

Arnold Schifrin is a young painter of great charm and self-confidence who has since made a small splash in the art world of California but who at that time was living here, gaily and with civilization, on little more than thin air. His wife Anne is tall, handsome, reserved, and serene. She was about to have her first baby, and Arnold had made a reservation for her in the hospital at Celaya. Several of the Schrifrins' friends had offered to take Anne there at any hour of the day or night, so that even if one or two of us happened to have car trouble or be out of town when the time came there would always be a car and driver on call. Anne seemed to be in good condition, and the only thing that worried all of us was that the date when the baby was expected was very vague.

One night we saw Arnold and Anne at the opening of a show of paintings at the Instituto, and at four o'clock the next cold morning there was a beating on our front door. It was Arnold, and he said that Anne's pains were coming hard every five minutes. He limped hurriedly home on his game leg while Peggy and I threw on our clothes and dashed for our car. When we reached Arnold's house, he was at the front door saying that I'd have to go for Dr. Olsina at once: he didn't think there was time for Anne to reach Celaya, some forty miles away. Peggy and Arnold went in to Anne, and I drove off to the doctor's house.

I was not very happy about this assignment, because Dr. Olsina usually goes to bed and rises late, and while he is a kind and civilized man he is not one to be pushed around thoughtlessly. His German shepherd dog Perla and then a sleepy maid admitted me, and then went to waken the doctor. While I studied the paintings, books, and framed Hippocratic oath I could hear the doctor grumbling and groaning in his adjoining bedroom. When he appeared he was distinctly chilly

in tone, and had a few remarks to make about women who
became entirely too excited entirely too soon. However, he
stuck one rubber glove in a pocket and came with me.

At Arnold's house he went into Anne's bedroom with
Arnold while I found Peggy in the kitchen trying to beat up
a charcoal fire to boil water and sterilize that glove. Soon
the doctor appeared and said that the baby would have to be
delivered then and there. He was calm and friendly now, but
Arnold was having kittens of his own. The doctor gave Arnold
and me a list of drugs and things to get from the drugstore
and told us to fetch also his nurse, Maria, who would bring
equipment from his office. We dashed off while I did a little
worrying of my own about Peggy. She had been a farmer's
wife, and keeps her head, but she is not very happy about
blood.

I beat on a window next to the drugstore, and after a
while a hand appeared and took in my list, through the grille,
without a word. Meanwhile Arnold had gone limping and
running down the street to waken Maria at her house. By
this time the sky was turning pale, a cloud or two was touched
with pink light, and the whole town began to glow and stir
in its sleep. A *campesino* came along carrying a little white
coffin and a bunch of flowers that he had bought somehow to
take back to the ranch. Fortunately he went around a corner
just before Arnold appeared with Maria. At last the drugs

were handed out of the window and we all dashed back in the car, over holes and cobblestones, to Arnold's house.

Meanwhile Peggy had been standing by Anne and Dr. Olsina. When the pains came, she held one hand while the doctor held the other, and he explained that that was why four-poster beds were good: you could secure a rope to the posts at the foot and the mother could pull on that. The doctor said that he had to have a string and a pair of scissors, both sterilized. Peggy turned the house upside down, but all she could find was a pajama cord and a pair of nail scissors; however, she managed to sterilize those. Luckily Anne had a rubber sheet. The doctor kept smoking cigarettes from a holder resting across the corner of a bureau without touching anything.

When we arrived and the nurse went into action with the doctor, Peggy heaved a few deep sighs of relief, made hot tea for all hands, and then waited with me in the patio. Anne's groans were strictly functional and quite without self-pity, but I was sweating for Arnold, too. Finally there was a pause, and then we heard a small, wailing cry of protest against the whole arrangement, and perhaps of relief. I've heard some good sounds in my life, and that was one of them.

Arnold appeared, weeping and grinning, and said that Anne was all right, the baby was a girl, and everything was wonderful. After a while Dr. Olsina came out and apologized to me and to Arnold for being rude that morning. "Anne is a brave girl, of good sense," he said, "and I am glad I was here." I caught a glimpse of Maria oiling the little red baby, and although that fine old woman must have helped with hundreds of babies, her face gleamed with wonder and delight. So did Peggy's.

When we went home to breakfast, the morning sunlight was very beautiful on the four-hundred-year-old town. I don't think that mankind will destroy itself for a while yet.

3.   THE SOUND OF WINGS

When the alarm clock stabbed me awake in the dark on that cold winter morning, I wondered for a moment, as always, why I was such a fool the day before as to agree, and even with enthusiasm, to go duck-hunting. By the time I had found a cigarette and a flashlight and hurried into my clothes, I felt much better about it.

"The thermos is full of coffee," said Peggy sleepily. "Good luck, and you all be careful with those guns."

"Thanks, we are," I said, and stepped out onto the little balcony above the patio. Orion had swung 'way over, and cocks were crowing, as they usually do from about midnight on. Groping my way downstairs with my gun, I tried to remember:

> *Some say that ever 'gainst that season comes*
> *Wherein our Saviour's birth is celebrated,*
> *The bird of dawning singeth all night long;*
> *And then, they say, no spirit can walk abroad;*
> *The nights are wholesome; then no planets strike,*
> *No fairy takes, nor witch hath power to charm,*
> *So hallow'd and so gracious is the time.*

And then that imaginative skeptic, Horatio:

> *So have I heard and do in part believe it.*

In the tiny dining room and kitchen, I snapped on the light and found the thermos. The coffee was hot and good. I found also the flask, and filled it with rum. Jamie, our black cocker, padded curiously downstairs, and I had to remind him that actually he hates the open country, so full of needly little burrs for his big feet, and that he wouldn't any more leap into a pond and swim for a duck than dive into acid. Jamie sniffed the butt of the gun, agreed, and padded back upstairs. Now that I was out of the way, he would leap on the bed and cuddle up to Peggy.

In the faint light from the lantern on the corner, and from the stars, our tiny dead-end street with its crumbling plaster walls, cobblestones, and burro dung looked like a stage setting on which might slowly appear, hooded and cloaked, the First and Second Murderers. On the steps of the little chapel at the corner, which everyone on our street uses as a kind of veranda, I sat down to wait. Those steps are well above most of the town: in fact, about on the level of the cross, its bulbs gleaming like jewels, that tops the Parraquia. The faint and scattered street lights did not extend far into the black, rolling country, walled in by the mountains.

Headlights of a car: yes, Leonard, dashing and bouncing up the hill in his station wagon. He is a stocky Canadian painter in his forties, with bright eyes and a thick mustache. For duck-hunting he has the enthusiasm of a boy. With him were Jack Baldwin, also a painter, slight, sensitive, and keen, and that young Mexican with thick shell rims, Felipe, who works in the post office. Everyone was now wide awake and eager to go. We had agreed that time to go out only a few miles on the Querétaro road, to one pond only, from which we could return by nine o'clock. Felipe had to be back at the post office by then, and the rest of us didn't want to spend a whole morning hunting, either. There is usually better hunting at the ponds beyond Dolores Hidalgo, but that's a considerable expedition.

We bounced over the cobblestones the rest of the way up

the hill — men with burros were on the streets already — and then out into the upper open country. When we turned off the road into a rough trail, the rocks and holes looked very large in the headlights, and the cactuses looked like grotesque figures in a frozen ballet. Around an adobe village where dogs barked at us savagely, on a little farther, and then we left the car, turned out the lights, and loaded our guns. After a short walk in silence we came up beneath a long, low, earthen dam topped with trees. Slowly we climbed it and then peered out across the sheet of perhaps ten acres of black water that sparkled a little. Already the sky was paling above the mountains to the east. On the far side we could see darker specks floating. There was a slight splash, then a couple of quacks. Thirty or forty of them, perhaps, and maybe there were more down at the far end.

We conferred in whispers. Jack would go down the dam to the left, towards the far end, and Felipe the same way, less far, while I should go down to the right, followed by Leonard. Soon I left him behind a bush and went on, crouching, out of the cover. Then we waited awhile to give the others time. The light was coming rapidly. It would be better if the ducks got up themselves, or Jack got them up with his spare .22, before they could see us well, but we couldn't wait until it was broad daylight. Finally I walked slowly, crouching, out across the dried mud and corn stubble, towards the other side of the pond. The chances of my getting within range before the ducks saw me were slight, but if and when I got them up, they might fly over the other men, still unseen. Well, they weren't mud hens, anyway, and looked big: maybe pintails. I slipped off my safety catch, and my heart was pounding. I figured Jack and Felipe must be ready by now.

After another wait I started forward again, on my knees. The ducks were perhaps nearly a hundred yards away. Not much chance, but still. Ai! With a splash and a whirr there they went, climbing fast. They broke into a larger and a smaller flock and circled, far out of my range, but two guns

spoke from the dam, and one duck plummeted into the water. Moments later, another shot: that would be Leonard. The larger flock, still rising into the light, formed a wedge and moved away until I could see them no longer. Off to some other pond, probably not to return that day. But the smaller flock, of seven, was coming down again and — yes — right my way, along the shore. I swung my gun up as easily and smoothly as I could. They turned — wham! — wham! No, damn it, both misses. One came right on, over my head, so that I could hear his wings. Ai ... ! And I have never found the right words for that sound. The smoking empties were out, and two new shells in, too late. Ah well.

I sat down on the dried mud cakes and lighted a cigarette. The sun came up singing, and the whole world was fresh. "But, look, the morn, in russet mantle clad . . . " It was Felipe who got that one across the pond. I could see him throwing a couple of rocks beyond his duck, trying to wash it inshore. No go. He was stripping to his shorts, and by golly, there was Leonard, too, taking off *his* pants. That water would be shocking-cold. Leonard had only to wade up to his knees but Felipe dove in, and there was Jack, too, watching him. I thought again of Dean Warnholtz, another painter who had had to go back to the States with that big black New-

foundland of his, a stouthearted, eager, intelligent bitch named
Roxy, who leaped into the water almost before the duck
splashed and brought it back without fail. My friends were
laughing and calling now. Leonard's duck was only wounded,
and it swam away, but he caught it and rung its neck. "The
poor little devil nearly got away from me wounded," he
called clearly.

Another gun: Jack's, and both misses, like mine. This time
the seven remaining ducks said, "The hell with this place,"
and departed for good. Not a thing in sight but three mud
hens. Slowly I walked back around the pond. Those ducks
might have come back, but we couldn't wait for them that
time. Two ducks were poor enough shooting by four men,
but that never seems to matter much. Even Lebrun and Pinto
had days without one duck to show for their shells. This
reminded me of that morning when Lebrun wounded a duck,
a great hawk dove and seized the duck in his claws, and
then, unthinking, I killed the hawk. It was a great savage
beauty of a bird, that hawk, and I felt sorry, as I never have
over a dead duck. Later a falconer down at Manzanillo told
me it was probably a peregrine: he said they fear no man or
gun. Now there came along an old man with a yoke of oxen
and with a burro carrying his plow. *"Buenos días, señor,"* he
called cheerily, and I called back. Good morning, good people,
good world.

Felipe had got his duck, all right, but was still shaking with
cold, so we hurried back to the car, the coffee, and the flask.
All of us talked happily at once about what had happened
that day and on other days of duck-hunting. Leonard had a
treat that time. From his car he hauled out a gasoline stove
and the food Reva had put up for him, and in a jiffy he made
us bacon and eggs that never taste that good indoors. One
duck is nothing, so Leonard gave his to Felipe. This courteous
and reserved young man had an old single-barreled gun, and
no shells to waste, like the gringos, and he's a better shot
than most of us. A small chicken can cost the price of ten

shells, so down here hunting ducks is different. When I get
some ducks, our Maria cleans them and Peggy cooks them
well, but what I like best is the soup. No: what I like best
is the sound of wings at dawn in a brave new world.

They dropped me at the little chapel at the corner of our
street, and we all agreed to go out together again soon. When
I came through the big green door into our cheery little patio,
with the garden freshly watered in the sunlight beyond, Maria's
bronze face lighted up, then fell. *"¡Ah, señor! ¿No patos?
¡Que lástima! Pues mañana es otro día."* And Peggy says, "Oh
dear, I had my tongue wrapped around a duck. Your bath
is hot, but come out on the terrace first for another cup of
coffee."

4.   CHILLS AND FEVER

One night not long before Holy Week, in Peggy's company
only, I discovered that I had been hurt by my friend Leonard,
and was very angry with him — or so it seemed at the time.
After Peggy went to bed, I sat alone on the terrace under
the stars with two more drinks and composed speeches to
him that seemed restrained but effective.

At four the next morning we got up to go out and see a
religious procession enter town. Leaving a friend's car in a
street, we crossed the little river with flashlights and scrambled
up a rocky trail between cactuses. Scores of dark figures
scurried by in both directions. It seemed to me, although not
to the others, very cold, with the stars dripping icy light
upon us, and I remembered taking star sights at dawn on
the North Atlantic.

As the sky began to pale, the procession of several hundred
people appeared in the distance carrying three life-size figures
shrouded in white and purple. The leaders were a group of
tough-looking men, respectfully hatless, with their heads

wrapped, pirate-like, in colored scarves. These kept singing a savage dirge and refreshing themselves from bottles in their pockets. One of the bearers was my barber, a handsome, ravaged young man who is mad about popular music and the bulls, and who, gorgeously uniformed and mounted, impersonates Ignacio Allende himself in our parade on the national holiday. Several times the procession paused while the figures were rested on tables under the arches of leaves and colored papers that had been prepared for them, and prayers were said. We few Protestant gringos on hand knelt out of courtesy, and once I found myself in the dust and dung beside a white-haired American gentleman who looked like a more intelligent Mr. Pickwick, who had been a big commercial executive, and who therefore, in relation to the needle's eye, was a camel like me — but of course a much larger one.

At the main arch, on a hillside facing the town, with hundreds of people gathered below and across the river, the figures were met by a priest, a small orchestra playing a lament out of tune, and forty-odd men and boys dressed like Roman soldiers under Aztec influence. While the music continued and fireworks exploded, there were more prayers. Just

as the first harsh, level sunlight touched the figures, at seven
o'clock, small boys respectfully removed their coverings, which
consisted, underneath, of personal scarves presumably loaned
for sanctification. The Christ, a realistic and bloody figure
in purple velvet pantaloons, was stooped over a pillar, just
having been brutally scourged. The grieving Santísima Virgen
and Señor San José were both relatively youthful. When the
procession moved onto the ford and across the river, the
raised figures, the lances and garish colors of the Roman
soldiers, and the hundreds of dark, grave faces were all
reflected perfectly in the still water.

We brought three friends home with us for breakfast in
the warming sunlight on the terrace. Maria, who had gone
out into the dark with us, had got home first, on foot, to
serve it cheerfully. When Leonard and Reva appeared, with
their dachshund puppy, Lucy Loosebones, to invite us to
dinner that day, I began to notice that I was lightheaded, and
that for me the pretty garden scene, with the friends and the
romping dogs, had no reality whatever. Soon after, I slept
a couple of hours in the sala, but awakened cold, with a fever.

However, we bathed and dressed and both went out to
dinner. For well people the food and company were excellent,
as usual at the Brookses', but for me everything was out of
focus. A young painter, accompanied by his adoring fiancée,
showed some of his drawings, which were sensitive and strong,
but he himself looked like a squirrel, and I kept expecting
to see his furry tail arch up over his back. A distinguished
portrait painter seemed to look and talk like an attractive
Tugboat Annie. A famous old actress fixed me with her eyes,
talked to me about God, and then told me a vivid story about
her youth in Sweden, with small boys leaping safely from
chunk to chunk of ice across a fjord. Leonard was a good
host, and he told me, in an especially friendly manner, to go
home to bed and stay there; but I was not quite sure that I
had ever met him before.

I took his advice, and the cool sheets were heavenly, but

the band music and the explosions continued all evening and night, and I dreamed about a religious procession crossing an ice floe. This time several people, including children, were drowned.

5. FEVER AND CHILLS

Dawn in Mexico can be much less agreeable than those so far reported here. So far Peggy and I have been remarkably lucky, but we have heard enough true stories to know that someday dawn may come at last to find us still in real trouble.

One night the commercial attaché at the Canadian Embassy was doped in his sleep and robbed in his own house. The Ambassador took steps, and soon after that the victim's landlord, a Mexican senator, was heard to say angrily over the telephone to some unidentified party, "You can't do this to anyone in *my* house!" Next the victim received a telegram to appear at a certain address, and when he went there, some stupid servant let him get a glance into a complete establishment for the reception of stolen goods, the alteration of car numbers, etc. His property was returned to him, and he was bustled out, but this outfit is still probably in business, with some degree of official protection.

An American Negro in the City had all the new furniture he had bought stolen from his apartment, and when he reported it he was himself imprisoned for several days as "a material witness." As usual, the American Embassy officials were completely indifferent — until someone pointed out to them that their attitude in this case would probably receive plenty of publicity, in both Mexico and the United States, as an example of racial discrimination. Then they acted fast.

More ordinary white Americans like ourselves, who also do not know any American senators, high officials in our State Department, or Mexican politicians or generals, would certainly be less lucky. It has been proved again and again that we can get into any kind of trouble, legally under Mexican law or quite illegally, without having any of our officials here give a damn. The British and Canadian embassies are much more helpful to their nationals, and even to Americans.

The problem, if it can be called that, is not a simple one. We Americans in Mexico are an alien minority, and because of the exchange rate a privileged one. It seems to me clearly up to us to keep our noses as clean as we can. If we do behave illegally under Mexican law, any attempt to escape punishment, or to get Mexican officials punished for doing their duty, would seem to me in bad taste, irresponsible, and dangerous to all of us. Any kind of "intervention" by "the colossus of the North" is now most clearly and happily — on the surface, at least — out-of-date. There are thousands of Americans in Mexico on our own volition, and I imagine that a fairly high proportion of us are eccentrics, drunks, neurotics, and so forth, apt to get into trouble. I can well understand why Embassy officials learn to hang up their telephones quickly and curtly.

On the other hand, it cannot be denied that corruption and bribery are rampant in Mexico, and civil rights almost unknown. By our standards, which are not so high as many Mexicans think they are, Mexican police and officials are informal, rugged, underpaid, and subject to all kinds of obscure temptations and pressures. Any of us can land in the jails, which are not pleasant, or be deported under armed guard tonight without explanation and without recourse. The money we spend here and the technical and other skills that a few of us introduce, on legitimate jobs, are important to the Mexican people. If we invaded Mexico in 1846, 1914, and 1916, it was the attitude of Lincoln and Seward that assured the triumph of Juárez in 1867, and it has been our armed forces, not the Mexican, that have kept Nazis, Fascists, and Communists out of Mexico. In short, I see no good reason why Americans should be pushed around in Mexico, or why, if something illegal and unjust is done to us, our Embassy cannot quietly and tactfully insist on our rights under *Mexican* law. If this resulted in more legal treatment of us than of Mexicans, maybe more of them would assert their own rights under their own laws.

All of these matters, and more, were involved in a recent most unpleasant incident, not in the metropolis, but right here in San Miguel. One night, without clear cause and without any legal procedure, the Mayor's secretary ordered the arrest on a street of two Americans and threw them into jail for the night. One raised a rumpus, and in the morning they

were released without explanation. Two leading Mexican citizens investigated the affair and forced the discharge of the secretary and an apology to the persons who had been jailed. The whole American colony and a few Mexicans became excited. Both claiming that they knew what had happened and why, one group asserted that the arrests had been legal and just, and that the discharge of the secretary had been a nationalistic, "extraterritorial" outrage, requiring a protest; while another group asserted that the outrage had been against the persons arrested, and that the secretary had been justly punished by Mexicans. Peggy and I and a few other people took a third position, that we did not know what had happened or why, and never should know, and that a protest by Americans from either side would in itself be illegal and dangerous. (Tacitly, and without any real evidence, we suspected that the secretary, the police, and the persons arrested had all been unconscious pawns in the hands of Mexican political forces engaged in an ancient struggle, between Church and State, that was none of our business.) As usual, for being skeptics, we were called cowards, but that didn't hurt us as much as others had been hurt. The ex-secretary opened a much-needed business for the collection and pasteurization of milk, and now there are only a few people still not speaking to each other. The possibilities of this little tempest in a teapot were considerable and dangerous, but on the whole, I think, both Mexicans and Americans in San Miguel showed good sense and came through it very creditably.

Recently, on a visit to the States, I got what was for me a new insight into the comparison of social order and violence in Mexico and the United States. The evidence was, alas, in no way new, but an actual episode has more effect than a newspaper story or columns of statistics.

I was seated at the bar in a coffee shop in Texarkana one morning when four young and middle-aged men, well dressed and with decent faces, sat down near me for coffee. They were salesmen, and after they had talked business for a while, I overheard the oldest of them, with a Northern accent, telling a story. I missed the beginning of it, but it went on something like this:

"So they got this nigger boy out in the middle of this pond that had all the statues around it, and they made him stay there. The water was up to his waist. The police come along, but when they seen it wasn't doing the nigger any harm they went away. So they kept him standing there in the water for twenty-four hours."

After a few halfhearted chuckles they went back to their sales problems.

When I thought then of some of the Mexican robberies, killings, and illegal imprisonments I had heard of, they seemed fairly sporting. The Mexicans have not governed themselves as long as we have, and they do not have the Anglo-Saxon legal and social traditions and inheritance of which we make so much proud talk. Don't talk to me too quickly about "Mexican barbarism," or about how well American Southerners understand and treat Negroes, and how long they need, still, to civilize themselves.

However all that may be, almost any dawn we can awake to find ourselves burgled, or shot, or in jail, or on the train, under guard, for Laredo. If or when the time comes, I hope we can keep our wits, our wills, and some sense of the larger picture.

6. LOOK!

As you see, even San Miguel can become as ingrown and infected as a college campus or a military post, but when this happens, all we have to do is to load the station wagon with our odd collection of traveling gear, which includes sketching materials, a reading lamp for hotels, and Jamie's gear, and so light out for strange and beautiful places where we don't know anybody and nobody knows us. Many of our friends go for this purpose to Mexico City, and Peggy enjoys that place too, more than I do, but what we really savor are the remote towns and villages and the dubious roads that may beat the bottom out of our car and leave us stranded. We are only

two days from the east coast or the west coast, and we prefer
the latter, but one of our most memorable jaunts was one we
made with Leonard down into the state of Vera Cruz. When
sometimes I lie awake at dawn here in San Miguel listening
to the cocks crow, the dogs bark, the burros bray, and the
bells ring for early Mass, I often think of one dawn on that trip.

We had climbed into misty pine forests and then plunged
down into damp heat, mango and banana groves, and jungle
thickets full of flowers, all clinging to dizzy cliffs, with range
after range of mountains beyond, and with clear torrents
pouring down into the bright blue lakes dammed up in the
ravines. Through Poza Rica, a rip-roaring new oil town, the
gas flares burning brightly against the vivid greens of the
jungle, and so on to Papantla, a hot and ancient town where
they played bingo all night in the square. Down to the coast,
where the Caribbean rolled slowly against the dunes, up into
the mountains again, across the Mal País, a savage area of
black volcanic rock near Jalapa, and down again into the
great plantations and cattle ranches of the hot country, where
the cumulus clouds towering up ahead of us had a different
look that I cannot describe and that they often have above
the sea.

Our destination was Alvarado, a fishing village on an
estuary south of the city of Vera Cruz, where Leonard had
previously had fun and good painting. However, except for
a boat trip up a river to the ancient cattle town of Tlacotalpan
— all blue and pink and green and empty, the dream of a
frustrated pastry cook, or perhaps of Chirico — we all found
our short stay in Alvarado very depressing. The swimming on
the outer beaches was good, but the sands were literally
burning-hot, so that I had to carry poor Jamie to and from
the car. Alvarado itself was now a dismal little town whose
life had all been sucked out by the main road south from Vera
Cruz. In the one small hotel the wife of the proprietor had
a mysterious fever, and so could not cook for us. All she
could do was sit in the main room in a dressing gown and

play solitaire. The proprietor himself, an American, lived only for his fishing and let anyone else worry about the water pump, so that usually there was no water, the toilets stank, and clouds of mosquitoes took over. We staggered out to wash and eat where we could, only to find that all the good fish that we saw everywhere were being shipped to Vera Cruz, and that in the gloomy cantinas even the liquor was expensive. Even the children in the streets had that glassy-eyed look of despair. Leonard fought to get a picture or two out of the place, but it must have weakened even his vitality, because the results were sweet little Impressionist jobs that he quickly concealed. My own daubs were spectacularly and morbidly bad. Jamie lay gasping wherever he could in the violent heat, and finally Peggy caught herself a first-class cold, with fever.

"Before we get the hell out of this dump, tomorrow," said Leonard, "there is one place that I want you to see at dawn." In the pearly gray light the next morning we made our way through a slum in the palm trees hung on the side of a cliff down to a broad, flat, sandy area by the bay, where men were burning charcoal and repairing boats and nets, and where children and vultures wandered about scavenging. Here there was no empty despair, but a cheerful enterprise in the getting of food. The beached boats, the nets, the human figures, and the birds all made wonderful drawing material — well beyond my skill, of course, but that rarely bothers me too much. From across the bay to the southwest there rose rapidly a very large and black cloud that made the whole scene even more weird and melodramatic. When I found him where he was painting — and well, this time — Leonard pointed to the northwest, where the sky was partly clear above a band of mauve-colored mist. "Look," he said, "Orizaba." I could hardly believe it. There, a hundred miles away, pale ocher above the mist and crowned with snow gleaming in the morning sunlight, was the great mountain.

I don't know what or who made all this, including little people scrambling for food or pictures, or why we are here

so briefly, or what it's all about. I certainly cannot see any good reason why anyone should be moved, religiously or even aesthetically, by a mass of rock that is a scarcely perceptible pimple on the skin of a minor planet of a minor star. All right, all right, I'm just childish, and very glad of it.

7. SMART'S MAGIC KEY TO SPANISH

After all this it may be necessary to observe that usually we do not get up and go running around the town or countryside, or even awaken, until well after dawn. Our small bedroom above the patio has large windows on two sides and open doors on the other two, so that usually Peggy has a covering over her eyes before I waken to town or household sounds. When I waken, Jamie gets off the bed before I shove him off and goes to his chair. Dragging on a bathrobe and slippers, I look unseeing at some friend's painting or print, or at a photograph of our trees and front pasture at home, or at a framed dog license issued to Peggy's great-grandfather, Charles

W. Morgan, in New Bedford in 1836, and then out across
the semi-desert and up at the sky. Then down through the
blooming plants in the sunlight and shadow of the little patio,
and into the bathroom.

These ten or twenty minutes before I am functioning well
are important to me. It is during this period that, if I have
misbehaved the night before, I feel keen and salutary remorse.
More happily, it is then that I think of good friends and happy
episodes far distant, of which I have not thought for some
time. It is then that I am most apt to see suddenly and precisely the elusive bad quality of what I wrote the day or week
before, and to attain a new concept or intuition of value.

It is because of the fluid and open quality of my mind early
in the morning that I once typed out and pasted up in front
of the john the complete conjugation, with 107 forms, of the
irregular Spanish verb *sentir,* and pasted up beside the mirror
a list of seventy-seven useful and difficult idioms. If you
remember your glasses in the morning, or are still young and
don't need any for reading, this trick has its uses, but of
course it is by no means the magic key that I am still seeking.
Someday someone else is going to make a fortune by dis-
covering and successfully demonstrating a method for making
the acquisition of new languages if not easy, then at least
less tedious and uncertain for all the poor devils, like most of
us Americans, who have little or no aptitude of this kind.

Peggy and I are fairly typical. In school and college we
studied some Latin, French, and German, but no Spanish. We
have lived in Mexico for four years. We consider it bad
manners and a waste of opportunity for pleasure to remain
too ignorant or crude in the language of our hosts. However,
as you can see, we have many good American friends here.
Most educated Mexicans are unsociable, and many are themselves trying to learn English, so that it is sometimes rude to
insist on speaking in Spanish. We can import American books
and periodicals freely, and there is no legitimate theater in

this town. Neither of us is in regular business, or involved in a love affair, with any Mexican. We do have some business transactions here, we like our neighbors and try to know them better, and we have taken regular lessons from time to time for months on end. Inevitably we know enough Spanish to get along in most situations without too much worry or confusion, but this is not enough. Just at the point when we might speak precisely and act decisively in some little jam, or might get some true insight and move into more articulate and important friendship, we are very apt to drop the ball. Despite our good teachers, we still have to force ourselves to do those damned exercises, when we do them, and we still drag ourselves to classes, when we do so, as though we were going to the dentist.

It is not that I retain any illusions about *easy* short cuts. No language records that I have heard seem to me to approach first base. From her *Magic Key to Spanish*, and from the report of a former student of hers, I should say that Margarita Madrigal was a born and fertile teacher, with new and useful methods for the beginner, but this book reaches almost its end before bringing up the really useful, necessary, and nasty verbs, constructions, and idioms. We go to the movies, when we do, partly in order to learn Spanish, but only a near emetic absorption of movies would be really effective.

The only hints that I have of a way out come from the year and more that I lived in France, knowing few Americans and reading entirely in French, and from my nearly four years in the Navy. In the latter, signals and other matters were beaten into my head day and night in a signal school. I taught myself, for the most part, how to navigate chiefly in order to escape boredom, and then I had to navigate quickly and correctly in order to keep myself out of the brig, or, for that matter, to keep my shipmates and myself alive a little longer. Could we combine the isolation with the language that I knew in France with some of the pressures for rapid learning and correct use that I knew in the Navy? Would it be possible to take a nearly lethal dose of language study, and so to get it over with for a while?

My "magic key," then, is a very rigorous "cure," taken for a few weeks or months as necessary, in a linguistic concentration camp that would be physically and perhaps socially as comfortable as the fees would permit, but that would be as isolated and as tightly governed as a naval training school. Other language groups would be broken up, even to the point of separating husbands and wives. Every moment of the day would be filled and controlled, with rebels fined and expelled at once. Every word would be spoken, heard, read, and written in the language in question. In the morning, severe monolingual classes and tutoring. In the afternoon, lectures, demonstrations, and concrete problem-solving in such matters as household construction, maintenance, and management; travel and automobile repairs; social intercourse and correspondence; gardening; business; law as involving aliens; banking; and high-brow, middle-brow, and low-brow conversation. Every night, a cultural lecture with pictures or a double-feature movie. Periodically, of course, searching examinations, with the flunks paying higher fees thereafter. Naturally there would have to be legal waivers and large deposits in advance, and armed guards and psychiatrists in attendance.

Ho-hum. Meanwhile my neighbor and friend, Don Carlos Quintanar, may step in for a chat, and if not, we can always pick up one in a cantina.

8. OUR MARIA

We have to distinguish thus because there are so many Marias.
When we come downstairs in the morning, our Maria, having
risen at dawn, gone to early Mass, and collected the milk
that friends very kindly pasteurize for us along with theirs,
is usually in the kitchen getting breakfast. She takes her
"delicious sleep," as she calls it, snoring and dead to the
world, in the room downstairs between the sala and the
bathroom that was intended to be a bedroom but that became
a catch-all, then an ironing room, and finally Maria's room
also. When she was evicted from her own house, we offered
her shelter until she found another, and last Christmas we
gave her a new bed. If we ever have enough money, and stay
here long enough, we shall build quarters for her. Meanwhile
she has her precious bed behind a screen, a cupboard full
of clothes mostly given her by Peggy, who is about her size,
a couple of cartons of her personal possessions, her rosary
hanging from a nail at the head of her bed, and her treasured
picture of the Santísima Virgen de San Juan de los Lagos.

Always in the morning her room is neatly made up before we appear.

When I come into the tiny dining room in my bathrobe, Maria and I exchange greetings and queries about any current little problem of health. We then consider the water problem, if there is one at the time, any unusual noises during the night, and any special Masses or fiestas that have caused an unusual ringing of church bells. Meanwhile Jamie has been clamoring for his milk and his toasted tortillas, and Maria now gives them to him, laughing at him tenderly and addressing him in a funny, polite baby talk that I can only partly understand. She is always amused by his hunger, and by our refusal to allow her to give him more than his ration. She says that if you eat without giving something to your dog the Devil is much pleased.

For Maria all our little jokes never wear out, and any little clowning and mimicry by me always makes her laugh happily for minutes on end. Once when she asked me whether I wanted a glass of cold water with my breakfast, I said. "No, thank you: water is for bathing one's self," and you'd have thought this hoary chestnut was a fresh masterpiece of wit. I still catch her chuckling to herself, *"¡El agua es para bañarse!"* (For use at parties attended by Mexicans, I have thought of collecting and translating in advance a score of Oscar Wilde's witticisms: they would be devastating.)

Maria has a short, sturdy figure with a beribboned pigtail down her back. Her finely cut bronze Indian face is enduring and even hard except when it lightens suddenly with this easy laughter of a young girl or melts in brief tears. She is perhaps thirty-five or forty years old, but I suspect that she does not know her own age and is not much interested in it.

It was when she was weeping once that I first really noticed Maria. At that time she was working for a friend of ours, an elderly gentleman then living briefly alone. Early one morning Maria appeared at our door, much agitated and in tears, to report that she had found her señor desperately ill.

We rushed downtown with her, fetched Dr. Olsina, and a few days later moved our friend, with his parrot and Maria, into our own house for his convalescence. At that time we had our own *criada,* Juana, but she and Maria were friendly enough, and after our friend went to Mexico and then the States, we kept Maria on. We then discovered that, for all Juana's skills and charms, Maria was the more reliable. When we were away, our tenants fired both girls, our friend Helen Wale kindly took on Juana, and we were left with Maria.

This affair of the tenants and the girls was instructive. We were going to the States on a lecture tour of some colleges, and there seemed to be no need for us to carry the house and servants while we were gone. The tenants were a serious young American painter, his equally serious French wife, and their pretty little daughter. They were obviously clean and responsible. After a few weeks Reva Brooks wrote us that the tenants had fired both girls and the part-time gardener, who was admittedly a poor specimen but the only man we had found to water the garden. With Juana rescued by Helen Wale, we had only to send money regularly to Maria, and we were very glad to find her waiting for us when we returned.

According to the tenants, both girls had been slack and insolent, insisting on doing everything not the way they wanted it done, but the way "La Señora Margarita" had always wanted it done. They said it was difficult even to move a stick of furniture. As for the gardener, he had urinated in the garden! According to Maria, the tenants had been stingy, harsh, and dishonest — and there was not a word of truth in this last, we happened to know. What it all amounted to was that the girls had not had the intelligence or will to adjust to tenants and that the tenants had not had the intelligence or will, and especially enough humor, to adjust to Mexico. This household was less difficult than most, and I doubt that these people will return to Mexico. If you are going to be grimly efficient and humorless about a house and servants you had better stay in the

States and pay thirty times as much in wages or do your own work.

It should be noted that these girls were being paid the equivalent of $6.40 U.S. a *month,* plus about the same in food, and some perquisites, for sixty or seventy hours of work a *week.* Maria is now getting $7.20 U.S. a month. The social and moral questions involved are not easy, and I don't pretend to know the answers. What I favor is pushing the privileged just a little harder than they enjoy, respecting and even "spoiling" the employed just a little more than seems wise, trying to see the whole picture with humor, and avoiding rigid theories and behavior and over-all "solutions." Always we have to keep our eye on what is happening to the individual human beings concerned, and that is never obvious.

It is certainly not clear in the case of Maria, an illiterate and very religious Indian who may leave us tomorrow for reasons beyond our capacity to understand and beyond her capacity or desire to explain. She cannot read or write or tell time from a clock, but she can memorize the costs of twenty items from the market, never cheats or is consciously cheated, and always knows the time closely from the church bells and the sun. By looking at the sky, sniffing the air, and considering the phase of the moon, she is a very good weather prophet. Expecting to return to Ohio after this "time out," and wishing neither to leave Maria penniless nor to pension her at that time, we once suggested a bank account to her, and offered to contribute to it regularly, in proportion to her own deposits. I had inquired at the bank and found that this could be done easily, with Maria using a thumbprint as a signature and free to withdraw the whole at any time without consulting us. Maria was not at all attracted, and much preferred her tangible new bed. Perhaps — though we doubt it — she has a pot of bills buried somewhere: if so, I hope it is secret and dry.

Maria came from a poor little ranch and was married to a man who was so brutal to her that even the Church separated them. She almost never speaks of her past or her future, but during the fiesta of San Miguel she stayed much in the house because she feared her husband was in town. Recently a letter arrived, addressed in her care to her mother-in-law, and she told us later without much interest that the rumor was that her husband was in jail in Mexico City: this letter, she said, might have been about that. Perhaps because she never had a child — or at least one that lived — she is oddly shy with children, and also strict about their manners, but never unkind. The failure of her marriage may have something to do with the fact that she has lost touch, it seems, with her relations, for this is very odd in Mexico.

She does have a few friends in town, and the younger of these, and many of the people on this poor little street of ours, often address her respectfully as "Doña Maria." We have had a string of funny little girls in a few hours a day to help Maria with the cleaning and ironing. They don't last long because they are always getting married or otherwise involved, but Maria says it is because nowadays none of the young girls want to work. Peggy always tells the new girl and Maria both that Maria is the girl's immediate boss.

Whenever I can, I have Maria buy the wood or whatnot from people selling wares at the door. She can get much better bargains than we can, and dearly loves the haggling. Respectfully she submits that the wood I buy is apt to be "garbage, and at a very high price." Our strawberry man is a wag and a wit worthy of all her powers, and the farce they put on — "Look, you had your finger on that basket when you weighed it!" — "Doña Maria, you know that I am the soul of honor!" — etc. — is really fun for all. But Maria may have spoiled this fun for a while when the other day she dragged the man and his berries into Don Carlos' store next door, borrowed the scales, and proved that he had tried to cheat her and us out of two hundred milligrams. From his angle that was carrying a good joke just a little too far.

We have long used a very good plumber who is now at

his request, because he likes the work, our part-time gardener, coming before and after his regular work. At two pesos, 16¢ U.S., an hour, he is relatively expensive, but good. Bathed and properly dressed, like a chairman of the board, he could be photographed by Bachrach and used as an advertisement. Once when Juana was working for us, we found him at the front door with his plumbing tools, locked out and in a towering rage. Juana claimed that he had made a pass at her. When he returned many months later, I asked Maria whether Juana had told her this story. She laughed and said noncommittally, "*Si, señor.*" "Well," I said, "I don't know what happened, but now that he is coming regularly to work in the garden, and often when we are not here, you know where my shotgun is, and I daresay you know how to fire it." "Oh yes, señor," she said, laughing merrily, "but if I need to I'll use instead your big knife. It would be much more convenient." More laughter, but after a little silence she added sadly, "It would be different if I were pretty."

The fact is that this tough little woman, who had, like most Mexican women, such tragic trouble with her man, and who is, I suppose, ugly in the conventional sense, although

she would be a marvelous model for a sculptor, dearly loves
the clothes that Peggy gives her, and spends her own money
sometimes on cheap perfumes and on such things as a bright
blue nylon blouse that, shyly, is her pride and joy. Once
Peggy gave her a nice suit, and she was delighted, because of
course a woman's suit, even more than a man's business suit,
marks an incredible leap upwards socially. Interestingly
enough, we have never seen Maria clothed in this suit. Peggy
thinks that she may carry it out and put it on in some friend's
house.

It was not in any such costume, but in the sturdiest, simplest
clothes that she had, plus a treacherous pair of saddle shoes
given her by Peggy's sister, that a year ago Maria set out,
across the river and the mountains, with hundreds of pilgrims,
on the great annual pilgrimage, in the dead of winter, to
San Juan de los Lagos, where the Virgin has performed so
many miracles. This is a walk of eight days, and the pilgrims
cook and sleep in the open. When Maria returned she was ill
at the home of an aunt for weeks.

This last winter, the day before we had to leave the
country for new tourist cards and were driving to Mexico City
to fly to Quatemala, Maria showed to Peggy a tumor on
her knee that was the size of a grapefruit. She must have had
this thing when she went on that pilgrimage — perhaps in
hopes of its miraculous cure. It was then too late to do anything about it, but we told her that something had to be done
as soon as we returned, in a fortnight.

When we returned we learned first from Reva — who had
the situation well in hand, as always — that Don Carlos
(whom she dislikes) had found Maria unable to walk and
stretched out on the sofa in our sala. She didn't even have a
fire because she said she didn't want to waste our wood. Don
Carlos summoned Reva, who got Dr. Olsina, who promptly
operated on Maria's leg in the wretched little town hospital
that everyone is trying to do something about. Although
serious and infected, the tumor was benign, and evidently

Dr. Olsina did a perfect job in removing it. Other friends helped, and Maria's mother-in-law had come in from the ranch to stay with her at night until we returned. One friend of ours, Sylvia Samuelson, had taken Jamie in, and he was fat and sassy and almost woundingly in love with his hostess. When we returned with guests we found not only Maria in this condition, but the garden parched and frozen, three pipes frozen and burst, and of course no plumbing operative.

Maria recovered rapidly, and since then she has been as merry as a canyon wren or *saltapared,* speaking respectfully and gratefully of Dr. Olsina's part in her cure, but more fervently thanking all the deities and saints, and walking a mile when she hardly could to thank San Antonio. This interested and puzzled us, because this saint's special province is getting husbands for women who for some strange reason want them. For the record, surgery, medicines, the hospital, a nurse all cost me about three hundred pesos or twenty-four dollars U.S. Maria sincerely asked me to stop all her wages until this was paid, and I am knocking off ten pesos a month for five months for her self-respect.

Clearly the Church gives to Maria all her faith, all the answers, all her science and art, and most of her companionship. Perhaps because she is only four and a half centuries from her Aztec or Tarascan ancestors, her thrills come from accidents and sudden death. "How sad! What barbarism!" she exclaims, and then goes into every bloody and physiological detail with zest.

Maria's attitude towards Peggy and me would be hard to guess. Peggy has her much more firmly in control than I do, and this commands her respect. Also, Peggy treats her with kindness, good sense, and tact. Once when Peggy was ill, Maria spoke of her to me as "a very noble lady." Whether I am anything more than a generous clown, I don't know. She likes it when I kill ducks, and even a little perhaps when I drink too much — though she would deny this vigorously, and has even, blushing red, lectured me on this subject. One

evening when I was a little high I went into Don Carlos'
store next door, and was introduced to a ranch friend of his
who had come into town on a handsome horse. When I admired this animal, I was invited to take a ride. I mounted and
went tearing up the hill on the Querétaro road, and then down
again. As is usually the case in Mexico, this horse was full
of spirit but perfectly trained, so that a child could have
done as much. When I came tearing down the hill, stopped
dead in front of the chapel, dismounted, and thanked the
owner I saw Maria standing in the shadow of our front door
and felt for the first time that in her eyes I might be *muy
hombre*.

I think that Maria finds it one of those acts of God in-
comprehensible to human beings that we have no children.
Of course we are gringos — a word she never uses — and,
much more serious, not Catholics. Besides doing cheerfully
almost all of our hard, personal work for so little money, food,
and so forth, I suspect that she prays that we shall become
Catholics, or if not, that our souls will somehow be spared
from Hell.

I can rarely remember Maria's last name, which she, of
course, does not know how to spell. What does that matter
to her? If she does what the Church requires, and is as good
as she reasonably can be, *the* Maria will care for her through
all eternity.

9. MORNING SUNLIGHT

When I am having breakfast, usually reading, with Jamie
under the table growling gently to Maria and me that he
would love just *one* more tortilla, *if* you please, Peggy floats
in cheerily in her blue dressing gown, greets everyone, and
begins to organize the day. Since I come to life in the morning
— to practical life, that is — rather slowly and resentfully,

much of this passes over my head. This can be annoying to
Peggy, of course, but unless some little problem really troubles
her, she accepts this tousled and remote husband who is,
after all, hardly a stranger to her.

Although enlivened by pictures, flowers, and a large round
mirror framed by a sunburst of bright tin, our dining room
is small and dark, so we generally wander out on our terrace
in the sunlight for a final cup of coffee. Peggy rarely lingers
over hers, because the garden and scores of potted plants are
spread out before her, a mass of little problems and challenges
to her green thumb. Meanwhile, unless I am called to action
by some workman or water problem, or merely by the necessity of acting as garden chambermaid to Jamie, I am wallowing
in the colors, forms, lineal and tonal patterns, textures, and
effects of light presented by that same garden and by the part
of the town spread out below it and merging into the rolling,
semi-arid countryside beyond.

On a balmy, sunny morning, such as most of ours are,
the detail is rich and various, and the total effect is warm and
cheering, "peaceful and exciting." If I had not become so
obsessed, and properly so, with the problems of pictorial
composition, which among us amateur painters "separate the
men from the boys," I think I could happily spend many
hours merely drawing both plants and their blossoms — both
copying them as realistically as possible and trying to invent
shorthand methods, appropriate to the pencil or pen or brush,
of suggesting their essential forms, qualities, and gestures.

Peggy must have a hundred different kinds of plants in
her garden, each with its own quality: the curving green
swords of the iris leaves, packed together and rising up around
the opulent formality of the flower that blooms almost any
time here and that inevitably suggests the Queen of France
in Burke's passage of purple; the bright little faces of the
pansies, like crowds of schoolgirls in their different uniforms;
the thin, virginal reserve and delicacy of the annual larkspur;
the hearty, almost blatant masses of the geraniums in all

their different colors; the cheerful little alyssum, planted along the walk but running wild everywhere; the extraordinary modeling and the wonderful cool gray green of the broccoli plants; the pinks, the carnations, the stock, the timidly clambering sweet peas; the half a dozen more exotic, semi-tropical plants, whose names I shall never remember; the odd shapes of the orchid plants, bound like prisoners to their chunks of tree fern against the stone and adobe walls, and sometimes putting out long, delicate sprays of flowers that I find more weird and beautiful than any sold in shops; my poor banana tree that I brought from Valle de Bravo and watered most carefully, rejoicing in the split forms of the leaves and in their murmur until deep frosts finished the tree off; the two delicate young jacaranda trees, with their feathery foliage, that will someday burst into airy masses of purple flowers; rising above the wall on one side, the delicate mass of our neighbor's mesquite tree, which we covet, the resting place of canyon wrens, hummingbirds, and the great noisy blackbirds on their way out to the fields in the morning or back to roost in the *jardin* in the evening.

I cannot skip the fine little roses, and the masses of zinnias, because I had an aunt who raised and loved these especially in the garden at Oak Hill in Ohio, twenty-four years and twenty-four hundred miles away; and because Peggy loved them after her, and now has them even here. They say that the chemists are now making new and brilliant paints, with which one will be able to equal even the colors of zinnias; good, but I have a long way to go with the paints that were good enough for the flower pictures of Renoir and Redon and Vlaminck. If I ever get around to flower pictures I think I'll set them outdoors, with gray flagstones, rich brown earth, and thick rugs of grass in sunlight and moonlight, shadow and mist.

Walking down to the low wall at the end of our garden, you will find that the whole thing is hung up in the air above the huge, ragged garden of my friend Don Carlos, and above this whole part of town, presumably like the Hanging Gardens

of Babylon. Those pillars of stone that make up part of one of our walls supported the roof of a little stable when our garden was a rocky corral. At the bottom of Don Carlos' garden those huge old maguey plants are the source of some of the pulque that his sister sells in his shop. Those ragged trees of his, rising pleasantly above even our walls, are heavy in the autumn with the best of English walnuts. On the other side there are ragged little yards and corrals, where dogs, cats, pigs, chickens, turkeys, and sometimes even horses wander about, ragged children play and sing, and old women go out to relieve themselves.

Out beyond, pleasantly punctuated by mesquite and a few other trees, including cypress, there is an area of walls and slanting or flat roofs in many different grays, ochers, pinks, russets, browns, and pale blues and violets, all running up the hill to the right, through tangles of nopal, to the tiny white chapel of San José, with its cypresses, which is the highest church in town. Although it is dangerously picturesque, a real painter could dominate this area and use it profitably for years. Out beyond, straight out from our garden path, where the North Star hangs oddly low at night, the countryside is ocher spotted with greens, and is rather dull except in the rainy season, when it brightens briefly into almost another Ireland. Mexico needs its mountains, which in that direction are only a thin blue wall on the horizon.

Back in the house, climbing the stairs out of the greenhouse patio, you can peek over the wall into the place of our one morose if courteous neighbor, an aging man who lives alone there, for the most part, and who, they say, brutally ejected his relations. They didn't lose much: two dark little rooms with earthen floors and smoke rising chimneyless through the tiles, one room a roofless well, and a dense little thicket of nopal cactus and bamboo. In Ohio most farm animals are better housed, and I suppose it is good for us to look over that wall from our luxury and to wonder. At this moment, however, let's remain would-be painters and go on up to the *mirador*.

In building the cistern and terrace out back, we had to eliminate the place where the laundry was hung out to dry, and so we had to provide another. A *mirador,* or looking-place, is merely a piece of roof, on or near the top of the house, with low walls and as many views as you can get. We had merely to strengthen the roof, build the low walls, and add

hooks for clotheslines. Although many Mexicans now have *miradors,* they seem to be valued more highly by us Americans. If they are agoraphobes, we are claustrophobes.

Our little *mirador* is rather breath-taking, I must say, with so much view that it is better for having a drink at sunset than for painting. From two sides the hill rises up steeply, with a mass of houses and trees and the bell tower of the school and convent of Santo Domingo. Below us, on the other two sides, there is spread out most of the town, a pinkish, russet mass from which rise a dozen really beautiful domes, bell towers, and spires that were built mostly in the seventeenth and eighteenth centuries, when San Miguel was a rich cattle town. Some of the baroque façades of the churches are visible too. If you look carefully you are apt to see a tiny figure or two of men or boys casually walking along the edges of roofs or climbing towers to ring the bells. Our painters have done interesting and of course very different things with all this: one turning it into a Persian carpet, for example, and another into forms floating on and reflected in water.

By this time the strong sunlight is flattening and deadening, pictorially, to the town and to the Guanajuato mountains out there beyond, but at dawn or dusk the forms emerge, the colors and tones are intensified, and the whole scene becomes vibrantly alive; and in the summer the great cumulus clouds, in all their subtle forms and colors, go very slowly through their esoteric ballet. I can see why the painters shun and dislike the vast blue empty skies of winter — what the devil can you do with them? — but, except once in a while for an El Greco effect, they don't seem to like clouds much better, and that I cannot understand so well. Ruysdael, Constable, Ryder, Matson, Marin, and many other undoubted masters have painted cloudy skies with plenty of "significant form" and emotion, and you can move the clouds around as you like. But, no: get out that damned old guitar, bottle, and watermelon.

But this is no time for arty argument. The pipes rising

from the corner of the *mirador* gurgle ominously, which
means that Maria has built a fire in the *calentador,* or hot-
water heater, down below some time ago, and that if the
water is not used quickly it will come spouting out on the
roof. Flowers, trees, and panoramas in the morning sunlight
are all fine, but for my taste a hot shower bath is one of the
few totally good inventions since 1492.

10. *DON CARLOS, MI CASA ES SU CASA*

During our six months' visit to San Miguel in 1949 we lived
in four different houses, and on our return in 1953 we lived
in still another for several months, and then for one month
in an apartment, before finding at last and moving into this
house. Presently our landlord, next-door neighbor, and friend,
Señor Carlos Quintanar y Nieto, wanted to sell it to us, and
when we showed little interest in buying it, he began to show
it to prospective buyers. Real estate prices in San Miguel were
rising steadily, as they have done ever since. We didn't want
to move again until we could return to our home in Ohio,
and with great good luck Peggy and I each had acquired a
bit of extra cash. The house is small, the newer part of it
was shoddily built, and there were water and legal problems
— the latter involving our status here as foreigners. The price
was about that of a good, medium-priced automobile in the
States. After renting the house for more than a year, after
much hesitation, and after consulting trusted friends experienced in business, we bought the place. We then had to spend
about eight hundred dollars more on necessary improvements
to the water system and on a new refrigerator. By this move,
which seemed more decisive and permanent than we think
it was, our families and friends in the States were startled and
perhaps dismayed, but they seem now to have accepted it.

I have never much enjoyed business, I especially did not look forward to it in Mexico, with my limited Spanish, and we had seen the Brookses and other friends here visibly worn down by such transactions and by the months-long process of rebuilding afterwards. Because in Mexico only men are considered fit to handle such matters, and because my Spanish was at the time slightly better than Peggy's, most of the job was mine. I hasten to add that she handles not only the operation of this house and garden, but also most of our banking and taxes in the States, while I handle those matters in Mexico. Within a few months we were both very tired of all the transactions, and especially of having the house torn up and workmen coming and going and making a racket all day long, but on the whole, we were agreeably surprised. Thanks for this fact are almost wholly due to Don Carlos, who, as a part of the deal, superintended all the necessary additions and repairs.

Don Carlos, as he is known respectfully and affectionately by everyone on our little street, is a very unusual and sweet-natured man. I thought at first that he probably seemed strange to me chiefly because I had never had such prolonged and important business to do with any Mexican, but then our friend Don Miguel Malo described Don Carlos and his family, whom he had known slightly for years, as "completely honorable, but also, unquestionably, very quaint."

Don Carlos is a short, plump man of about forty, a diabetic, but of great quiet stamina. He has unruly black hair and, like many middle- and upper-class Mexicans, he does not shave more often than he must, and in his case his beard comes out in odd little patches. He wears rimless glasses all the time except when reading, and then he takes them off and draws the paper very close to his eyes. At this time both of his lenses had been shattered and then patched together with some kind of gum or glue and tape, so that his eyes were almost invisible and it was hard to guess how he ever saw anything himself. Don Miguel told me that Don Carlos'

glasses, to his certain knowledge, had been in this condition
for ten years at least.

Once a friend of ours, a Canadian painter, had a show of
his work at the Institute, and these paintings were very
abstract, with beautiful, misty forms seeming to dissolve into
each other. Don Miguel, who happens to wear very thick
shell-rims himself, went from one picture to another mur-
muring, "Very subtle, very delicate," and so on. Finally he
said to me, "Señor, I have discovered the secret of this remarkable work. The painter has borrowed the glasses of
your friend Carlos Quintanar!" When I ventured to repeat
this remark to the painter, he was not amused.

I did not then venture to repeat the remark to Don Carlos
himself, but I honestly think that he would have enjoyed it.
He loves every kind of little joke and humorous saying, even
when directed at himself, and when he is amused, his rather
heavy, melancholy face lights up most happily. When the
sale and purchase of this house had been completed, and all
of Don Carlos' heavy mortgages canceled, he bought, to
everyone's relief, a new pair of glasses. A few weeks later,
however, his small son broke the new ones, and once more
he disappeared, if less completely, behind the gum and tape.
I hope this is not symbolic: I hope the mortgages have not
returned also.

In the huge, rambling old house next door, with the little
shop in the front entrance, Don Carlos lives with his plump
and pretty little wife, his handsome little son, his mother, and
his two unmarried sisters. Don Carlos' younger brother and
his family live in the next house down the street. The old
mother is a matriarch, but I think it is Don Carlos who has
to figure out how to finance the whole crowd. With all these
women on his hands and in his hair, and I suspect without
many close men friends, he is perhaps somewhat restless, but
of course the Family is supreme, and probably no change is
possible.

All of these people are extremely ingrown and self-sufficient.

Socially the family is at least as good as many in San Miguel
that put on many more modern airs and graces, but the
Quintanars never go out anywhere and never entertain. Don
Carlos told me once that his father had been politically very
active — I think in some conservative faction — during the
Revolution and had suffered disastrously. Don Carlos himself
dabbled in politics a few years ago and again lost more than
his time and his labor. When we talk politics, it is with as
much reserve on his part as interest on mine, so that I am
far from sure, but my impression is that he is a splinter-
party conservative of some sort, perhaps a liberal Catholic
hoping for the breakdown of the one-party domination by the
PRI, and hence, paradoxically, a sort of radical. In his relations with individuals without money or education he is more
generous and respectful than many Mexicans I know, but
he thinks we spoil Maria, and she knows and resents this
opinion. He told me once that God gave each of us what
little character and intelligence he has, and that sometimes we
have to accept our superiority as well as our inferiority, and
act accordingly. At least, that's how I understood it. It may
be that this odd little man behind the glasses is an old-
fashioned aristocratic radical democrat, and if so, that's all
right with me. Whatever he is, he doesn't seem to fit very
well into modern Mexico.

The disdain, if it is that, that new-rich Mexicans in San
Miguel, and others, may feel for the Quintanars may come
in part from Don Carlos' record in business, which has been
erratic. The little shop in the entrance to their house, where
they sell cigarettes, soft drinks, candies, soap, and a few
other articles, keeps the two sisters and the mother busy, and
may bring in a very little regular income, but that's all. Don
Carlos operates the remnants of a ranch left by his father, so
that men are always coming and going with corn, milk, farm
implements, and so forth, and burros are often parked in our
little street. He is interested in soil analysis, hybrid seed corn,
better livestock, and so forth, and is now dreaming of wells

with pumps, and irrigation, which would increase the value
of his ranch many times. In all this, however, he faces the
almost insuperable difficulties in getting credit that keep down
all but the very rich. Interest rates in Mexico, even on
government loans, are outrageous, running from 10 to 40
per cent. Don Carlos' wife is the skilled and energetic daughter
of a baker, and last year they set up a bakery in their cellar,
selling the products in what used to be a sala near the shop.
The bread is excellent, and perhaps a little too cheap. In
addition Don Carlos invented a new kind of cheese that he
makes with the milk that comes from his ranch. This also
is very good, and recently he received from an American
wholesaler in Mexico City an order for this cheese much
larger than he can ever fill. Here again the same question
arises: borrowing money at these rates, can he pay the interest
and capital and get over the hump? Don Carlos is as ingenious,
resourceful, and tenacious as he is dangerously kind and
perhaps gullible. He is the kind of man, familiar in all countries, who always has a scheme, who may become rich, and
who may slip steadily down into ever more severe but cheerful
and dignified poverty.

Peggy's and my relations with the Quintanar family were
good before we subjected them to the strain of buying this
house, and they have survived even that. They are always
very formally courteous with us, and we try to be the same
with them. When I ask for Don Carlos and am invited into
their house, I am always shown into the huge, dark sala,
which is full of elaborate cane furniture, religious pictures,
and musical instruments. Most members of the family play
at least one instrument, and until one brother, the first
violinist, died, they had an orchestra. When Don Carlos
comes to see me he always apologizes for interrupting my
work, shakes my hand on coming and going, and asks permission to go through a door or withdraw. There is a constant
exchange of potted plants between Peggy and the old lady,
and they keep sending us also little gifts of special cakes,

pulque, and even the most excellent pork from the ranch. Whenever we make a trip we always try to bring something back to the little boy, Carlitos, who is a very intelligent, sensitive, and cheerful little creature, in some danger of being spoiled by his family, the Smarts, and the whole street. Beneath all this there is, I think, a deeper bond between Don Carlos and me that I cannot well define. It may be that we are both eccentrics, improvisers, and displaced persons, but try to be honorable ones.

When the transactions began, I felt the need of a bilingual agent, and secured one who also managed for Don Carlos the cancellation, in Mexico City, of his mortgages. For these services my man charged us both, and especially Don Carlos, more than we thought just, and he also did not quite succeed in concealing the contempt he seemed to feel for my friend, whom he had known when they were boys. We had to pay and shrug off the bills, but Don Carlos and I were thus drawn more closely together, and were both glad to get rid of the agent, a large man with great black moustaches, whom I had introduced into the business. This was a cultured and attractive man, whom I still enjoy, but oddly enough, he just didn't fit into this picture. Another person who did fit in perfectly was my friend Jack Baldwin, whom you will remember going duck-shooting that morning. Jack very kindly consented to

become the legal owner of this house until I could obtain the
paper necessary to own it myself.

Only one problem came up between Don Carlos and me.
To help him out in a pinch, I had already paid a year's rent
in advance, without interest or discount. I had to pay for
the house in installments, and Don Carlos asked for high
interest, in the interim, on the unpaid amounts. When I de-
murred, he came up with a surprising suggestion from his
mother, the owner of the house: if I didn't want to pay this
interest, they could, instead, remove the stove from the
kitchen! All of this involved many hours of quite friendly
conversation, and Don Carlos finally admitted what I had
long suspected: that he saw my point and agreed, but his
mother did neither. I still refused to pay the interest, but in
our final settlement I made a small payment to Don Carlos
for his services, which had saved me much money, in super-
intending the reconstruction. The mother accepted this deal
and we all laughed the trouble off.

Meanwhile, to my astonishment, this little tangle produced
another event that still warms and touches me. This is a very
small town, and somehow Don Miguel Malo, who has already
appeared and will reappear, heard of my problem of the
interest. I didn't think he should know anything about it,
but there it was. One morning on the street downtown, in
front of the bank, this gentleman took me aside and told me
what he had heard. It should be noted that Don Miguel knew
nothing about me, morally or financially, and that, although
or because an aristocrat, he is by no means a rich man. He
proceeded to say, most courteously and delicately, that it
embarrassed him to think that I should be embarrassed in
this manner by my friend Señor Quintanar — "undoubtedly
a very fine man, but a little unworldly, a little eccentric, and
subject to family pressures" — and if I should be so kind as
to accept his offer, and not consider it crude on his part, he
would be most happy to loan me ten thousand pesos, without
interest, for six months. This was no mere gesture: he wanted

to step inside the bank and hand me the money at once. Well! I didn't have to accept this handsome offer, but I kept thinking that none like it had ever been made to me inside or outside a bank in my own home town, where my ancestors and I have paid our bills for 118 years.

The passing of the papers took place in our sala one evening, and was quite a scene. Those present were Don Carlos, his mother, Jack Baldwin, my agent, a local lawyer who had actually made out the papers, Peggy, and myself. The lawyer read every word of the long documents in rapid Spanish, of which I caught only the odd fragment, such as the reference to Jack as John Baldwin McGrath — using his mother's name last, in the Spanish and Mexican style. For me, and perhaps for others, the signing had a melancholy overtone. Don Carlos and his mother wanted to sell the house, and were delighted to get rid of their mortgages and debts, but here was the actual moment when one more piece of the property left them by Don Carlos' father was slipping out of the family hands. I kept thinking about little Carlitos, who might have inherited the house, and also about a farm in Ohio — the deed signed by Thomas Jefferson — that my sister and I had had to sell during the war. When the signing was completed, Peggy offered everyone wine and cake, but with the most elaborate courtesy and regret, because of illness, the old lady declined, and the others did the same. Jack remained after the others had gone, his wife Bunny came in, and the two of them put on a gay and ribald act of instructing us in the proper decorum to be preserved in *their* house.

A few weeks later, in Jack's class in lithography, I made a lithograph of our patio, looking through it from the front door and out into the garden and landscape beyond. Because of a clumsy accident I got only ten prints. The best one I had specially framed, with an inscription to Don Carlos, and gave it to him. It is now hanging in a place of honor among the family photographs and religious pictures in their sala.

Now that Don Carlos has been completely paid, his kind-

nesses have, if anything, increased. When Maria was taken
so ill during our absence, it was he who found her and called
our friends. After getting a new source of water, and building
a cistern and a tank, to make our house independent of Don
Carlos', we found the new source adequate for months, and
then *it* failed. At this point it was Don Carlos who suggested
connecting our house again with his and using half of whatever
water came into his house from the old, unreliable source,
the convent up the hill. How many people in San Miguel or
anywhere else, themselves short of water, give half of whatever
they have to a neighbor? One day, unknown to me, our
gardener blandly took our hose and siphoned into our cistern
Don Carlos's largest tank. Don Carlos just laughed.

As always in friendship, one never knows what will happen
next. Meanwhile from that house next door there issues and
floats up our little street a fragrance that is much more rare
and sweet than that of *huele de noche,* and that is the fragrance
of eccentric kindness and good taste, of intelligent, self-
respecting, and humorous humility.

11. THIRTY-TWO TO EIGHTY CENTS A DAY

Except the very poor, who have to let their houses crumble
over their heads, most people in San Miguel, both Mexican
and American, have had workmen in their houses, and the
tales about these men range from mere eccentricity and
drunkenness through burglary to rape, whatever that is.
Leonard Brooks had a maestro who could carve very well in
wood and stone, and who could have done very well selling
the bas-reliefs in the pale green stone of Guanajuato that he
carved from Aztec designs supplied to him by Leonard if
he had not preferred, like most good craftsmen, to execute
his own creations, which were realistic and dull. Probably
because they were hired and directed by Don Carlos, the

men who worked in our house were mild enough, but they still haunt me.

The maestro, who took orders directly from Don Carlos, with as little interference as possible from me, was named Francisco, or Pancho, a tall, thin, lugubrious man with very gentle manners and voice who worked very steadily. The others, too, spoke very gently, in murmurs, and I kept contrasting their voices and their manners with those of other workmen I have known, such as sailors and Seabees. I'd have felt better, somehow, if these men had cursed and slammed around a bit more. My impression was that Pancho had great traditional skill in stonemasonry — if not so much in concrete — but fairly low intelligence. Whenever he made a mistake he calmly took apart whatever he had done and did it over again. He got ten pesos, or eighty cents, for a nine-hour day — from seven to five, with an hour out, from ten to eleven, for *almuerzo,* a combination of breakfast and lunch.

The second man was much younger, a gentle, handsome fellow named Cándido; his skill was at least as great as that of Pancho, for whom his respect was marked. His wages were eight pesos a day. As helpers these two had two other men at six and four pesos a day each. One of these was a very small, elderly and tough man named Felíz, who wore the crown only of a felt hat, which I assume is much more comfortable that a stiff straw hat when one is carrying loads on the back. This Felíz looked, except for his small size and the darker color of his skin, remarkably like my old friend and classmate, Murray Pease, now director of the Conservation Laboratory at the Metropolitan Museum of Art. I used to sit staring at Felíz in wonder, recalling happy days at Harvard thirty years before. The other helper, at four pesos, was a ranch boy who was always overcome by shyness except when, finding himself on a roof outside a bedroom window, he would stare in frankly until I drew the curtain or waved him away. Perhaps he had the impression that the glass was of that special kind, used by detectives and voice-correction experts, that permitted him to look in without being seen.

This gang arrived soon after seven in the morning, and when it was cold, we had Maria serve them coffee and tortillas. She always kept them firmly in hand. They addressed her politely, and when they had to pass through any part of the house, she made them put down sacks and wipe their feet. When I appeared at about eight, usually conferring with Don Carlos, they all took off their hats and wished us good morning while the maestro went on to express the hope that we had passed a good night. I never did become used to this, or to the somewhat feudal nature of the whole relation, of the whole operation.

The core of the job was the building of a cistern between our back door and the garden to collect the water that from the new outer pipeline, as from the old, ran, when it did run, only intermittently and with no pressure. Also necessary was a concrete tank on the roof, with an automatic float valve and with an electric pump down next to the cistern, plus all the necessary pipes. As everybody knows, no such job can be limited: it always seems to be just the time, and more economical, to do a little more. We put a walled and flagstoned terrace above the cistern, with broad steps running down to the garden, and had the garden path flagstoned also. This meant demolishing an ugly wall that cut off the view. On the back of an envelope Jack Baldwin had sketched this terrace, but one morning I found myself confronted with the problem of telling Pancho exactly where to put the steps and the walls. I had tried my hand at a good many things, but never architecture. There was now no place to hang the wash, so we had to make a *mirador* on the roof. The water paint was peeling off the woodwork in the house, so without enough sandpapering this got one or two coats of dark green oil paint. Meanwhile we wanted an electric refrigerator, but there was not enough room in our tiny kitchen until we had a deep niche cut out of a stone wall three feet thick, and

then plastered, and the whole kitchen and dining room painted. There were now many other possibilities, but our bank account and our nerves had reached the end.

Next to the native skill of these men, what impressed me most was the fact that human labor was never considered, and almost no mechanical devices, however simple, were rigged up to take the weight off the backs and limbs of men. They carried stone, bricks, cement, sand, gravel, and lime through the house on their backs, with never a wheelbarrow or a murmur. When the big concrete tank was being built on the roof, three stories up, Felíz and that boy scrambled up ladders and boards and across roof tops with every single pound of the materials on their backs. To Pancho I managed to suggest a block and tackle, with sling, down the back side of the house, and offered to pay for it if he wanted it. "That might very well be possible, señor," admitted Pancho sadly, "but it would be very expensive, and who knows when we should ever be able to get such a thing?" They have them right here in town, of course, but I dropped it. Later Don Carlos told me that

these men distrusted the simplest gadgets and would rather
stretch out their work time than have it made easier but
shorter.

The whole job lasted about three months, and during the
first two everyone worked with a will. There was then a
perceptible slackening off. This annoyed Don Carlos more
than it did me. He said that work was then scarce in San
Miguel and on the ranches, but in his view, this wasn't a
good enough excuse. Then one evening I saw the sober,
correct Cándido pie-eyed on a street downtown, being held
upright by some friend. A few days later Felíz did not show
up. Sadly Pancho made that funny little gesture of a hand
tipping up a glass and said that Felíz was in jail. Incidentally,
Dr. Olsina tells me that all these arrests and imprisonments
for drunkenness are strictly illegal if the drunks molest no
one, and that the men are usually robbed by the police.

The last act came just a few days before the end of the
job, when Pancho himself failed to reappear after his *almuerzo*. About five o'clock that afternoon I was working in
the garden with Peggy, Maria was washing clothes in the
pilas, and the other men were finishing and cleaning up when
an odd silence fell over the scene. When I looked around
I saw old Pancho weaving uncertainly on the top step of
the flight of stairs he had so soberly and lovingly built.

"Patroncito," he gurgled, "I had one little cup too many,
and I am overwhelmed with shame."

Then he nearly fell down the steps. I managed to catch
him, told him it happened to everyone once in a while, and
led him through the house and out the front door. When I
asked Cándido, he assured me that Pancho would be able to
get home unescorted without being grabbed by the police.
There was not a smile, or a word on the subject, from anyone
present. When a new house is completed and blessed by a
priest, or when the builders are celebrating the fiesta of San
José, the activities and results are more spectacular.

At the end of a long job a tip is indicated for each hand,

and after consulting Don Carlos, I secretly made the percentage of wages slightly higher than he had suggested. On that last Saturday evening, to which we had all conspired to stretch the job, Peggy and I and Maria were all deeply relieved to have the job finished, and all those men and all that dirt and noise out of the house, for the time being.

However, Peggy and I have kept on thinking and talking about those men, and about the families being raised somehow on those wages, which are not steady at that. It should be noted that the cost of living here is roughly a third of that in the States, but even when you multiply these wage figures by three you don't get much money for a family. Then there is another consideration, so statistical and so brutal that I try to forget it, but can't: if you could suddenly double the wages of workmen in Mexico, and could suddenly cut the dreadful rate of infant mortality in half, you would produce wild inflation, a "population explosion" such as has never been seen anywhere, and political and social convulsions, bloody ones, of a kind with which Mexico is already much too familiar. I don't know the answers. If you do you might write them to President Adolfo Ruiz Cortines.

On a wall in the garden we found a memento: a small wooden cross, very crude, made out of a short piece of limb, with two of its own twigs projecting from it at right angles. Charming, of course, but I take it that Jesus, who worked as

a carpenter's boy for perhaps four pesos a day, didn't leave
that work for preaching, healing, and death in order to charm
anyone. Yet when I read what He is supposed to have said
about work, money, violence, and so forth, I find myself, like
other comfortable dullards before me, fascinated but not much
enlightened.

12. SHOP TALK

When we don't have any workmen around needing answers
or making too much noise, and when Peggy doesn't need immediate help with some domestic problem, right after breakfast I come up here to my small study to work. The views
from the two windows are superb, and at eleven o'clock Maria
appears with hot chocolate and crackers. For four or five
hours, with perhaps two or three more added later in the
day, I don't have to think about anything but my work. For
the time being, probably short, I can use my best energies
in this way without caring too much whether this writing
earns much money or not; and, what is more important to a
writer, I know, in making the final revision of this particular
job, that these words will be printed and read by a few people,
at least, through the years and after I am dead. With luck, I
may have another twenty or thirty years of this severe and
enchanted work or play. I may even, someday, at last, write
something really good. In all this I am joyfully aware, with
a tinge of fear, of my extremely good luck.

It has not always been so, and it will not always be so,
and this statement of my present situation opens up a little
shop talk that is relevant to the basic theme of this book.
Whether he is as lucky as I am at the moment or not, any
writer has to deal constantly, until he gives up writing or dies,
with four problems that all affect each other: (1) How is he
going to earn a living while writing — an activity that de-

mands his best energies and yet is not apt to keep him out of penury? (2) Money aside, how is he going to keep on writing, or give it up, when his work is not even published? (3) How is he going to find his best vein at the moment and keep growing? (4) How is he going to do the job in hand as well as he can do it? The last two questions are clearly the most important, and will receive the most attention here, but the first two cannot be brushed aside cavalierly, as they often are by successful writers or by critics on salaries.

Like most writers, I have held a good many different jobs and earned most of my living by doing other kinds of work than writing. In different degrees and ways each of these jobs has enriched and impoverished my writing mind and has deprived me of, or given me, enough time and energy for writing. Literary hack work can be instructive and amusing, but it is risky too, and should not be relied on too long. A country gentleman's life is good for this purpose, but obsolete. Farming has been industrialized and demands all of one's energies, as well as large capital. Military service, at least during a war, is too exhausting at the time, and for internal reasons that remain obscure to me, I for one have not yet been able to write well about it. I have found teaching, and the academic life, very congenial, but too critical and intellectual, and making a constant drain on mental energies that are too close to the creative ones. We are now living on income from capital in part inherited and in part earned, and the latter is more comfortable to persons of my social temperament. This is a very good solution, for me perhaps the best, but it adds severity to the second problem, that of successful publication, because who wants to be a privileged and total amateur? For the businessman in writing, the writer who carefully produces good merchandise and lives on it, allowing personal vision and art to take their chances, I have great respect and envy, more than for most "dedicated spirits." However, whenever I make a serious attempt of this kind, my agent and the editors sigh or laugh their heads off. All

I can do in this direction — and I think this is a good idea
even for more heavily endowed, high-brow, and dedicated
writers than I am — is to try to communicate with imagined
readers of taste and intelligence, and I think there are a good
many of these. What this whole problem comes down to is
one of scrambling along, as honestly, alertly, resourcefully,
and cheerfully as possible, while keeping one's material desires
to a decent minimum.

The second problem, that of successful publication, is apt
to seem minor only to the very successful or to those who
feign, or have actually attained, indifference to communica-
tion, and to functioning as professionals. Beginners, and
middle-aged old pros like myself, intermittently published,
still without solid reputations, and wondering whether medi-
ocrity and abortions are worth the long scramble discussed
above, are bound to be interested in this matter. The beginner,
self-confident but often baffled, can only go on producing,
experimenting, and studying the external results and his own
working mind. Given some real talent, he is often more
welcome in the market place than the old pro without a
solid national and international reputation, and he can be
spoiled and deceived, chiefly by himself. As an old pro of this
kind I can only say that I have found myself, with a kind of relief, beyond "the point of no return," beyond the possibility of
turning seriously to other work, and that I have made a
severe and prolonged effort to care less and less what happens
to my work after I have done it as well as I can do it. (Incidentally, this highly difficult and sensible effort is easier for
painters and sculptors than it can ever be for writers and
composers, simply because a painting or a statue *exists* in a
way that a MS or a musical score does not. At the same time it
must be admitted that a book, in a few thousand copies
kicking around in dirty old stalls and stores all over the
world, has more life than any but the most reproduced of
paintings.) In this effort I have not yet reached the admirable
if sincere point of sealing the only copies of my best MSS

in bottles and tossing them into the sea, and I was frankly much relieved and pleased when a publisher offered me a contract for the present book. However, I can say that I wrote it with less hope than I have ever written anything, and with as much care and pleasure; and also that except for their effect on sales, and hence on my agent and publisher, and except for what I can learn from them, which is more than most writers admit, I don't think I shall be much interested in the reviews. In other words, one can learn, if too slowly and painfully, that a good writer is no more important to himself than a good farmer or sailor, that MSS, like crops and ships, can be lost without stopping the human adventure, and that we are all, including Tolstoy and Shakespeare, going to be very dead very soon.

The really important problem is of course the third, that of finding one's best vein and continuing to grow. If this one, in my experience much the most difficult, is solved, the others are apt to take care of themselves, or if not, to shrink in importance. In my opinion, all of my MSS, except one, that have been rejected have richly deserved it, and if my best book (as I judge them) has made the least money, it has attracted the most important readers for the longest time. And when a writer is truly "in the groove" in the way that I mean, the more superficial, technical problems become a delight, and he can even be an attractive husband and friend, which he is certainly not apt to be otherwise. Every case history of this kind is unique, and to other writers interesting, but I don't write just for writers, so I shall make mine very short. Non-writers can read this whole chapter as a part, perhaps the core, of this record of an attempt to remain alive as an outsider, partly discarded, in a foreign land. For example, a retired financier living in Mexico might find his salvation not in amateur photography, but in going to his little room every morning and reconsidering, at length and in depth, the relations between politics, economics, and the individual human being.

By the phrase "finding one's best vein and continuing to grow" I mean attaining and maintaining one's unique personal vision of life, one's clearest, strongest, and most sensitive state of mind. Since this comes from the relation between the conscious and the unconscious minds, which are still so little understood, there are no useful guiding rules applicable to more than one person, and I doubt if there ever will be any. Each writer can only produce, experiment, and study the results as alertly and honestly as possible. In my case I am apt to "think" too much, too rationally, and too early in the process, and I have learned to value prolonged and concentrated "brooding," with special attention to the fringes of consciousness and to the emotional quality of the dimly adumbrated final product.

It may be more helpful if we turn to the choice of medium and subject matter, remembering that these choices, too, should come from the unconscious, with conscious clarification rather than direction and interference.

Like too many other writers, I drifted into fiction and produced four published novels and a play (a special case, commissioned and successfully produced and published by Ohio University), plus a long narrative poem and two bad novels, all three stillborn, before I finally admitted, here in Mexico, that although I had some deceptive talent in fiction, or I could not have gone this far with it, I was not really a storyteller at all. I watched people, including myself, with fascination, I could daydream about them happily and with some fertility, I loved and venerated a few masterpieces of fiction, and I studied the technical problems with delight, but as a storyteller I had one fatal deficiency: I did not really believe that my fictional daydreams, my "created" characters and stories — or indeed any others except a very few from the masters — had true validity and importance, or were as interesting as almost any actual human being or story I encountered. Several times I have thought that I might, however, be able to write civilized "light fiction," which I enjoy reading, when I can find it, but here also, when I tried it, I failed somehow to let myself go, and the results fell between two or three stools. The fact is that the true storyteller, of any kind, has to be absolutely convinced — as I have not been since I wrote my first very green and clever novel — that stories, and especially his own, are more interesting and important than actual life. There are worse mistakes to be made than writing a lot of novels without being a novelist, but this one has cost me a good deal, manifested in duodenal ulcers.

All through this experience, extending over twenty-five years, I have had to admit that I'd rather read a biography, autobiography, memoirs, journal, or letters, by or about almost anyone in almost any time or place, than almost any but a score of pieces of fiction of personal importance to me. With dreadful brass, justified only by the result, a work of art and scholarship, I talked my friend Paul Murray Kendall out of writing a novel on the subject and producing instead his definitive life of *Richard the Third*. When I read this enthralling book last Christmas in its first, English edition I had then to ask myself again why I did not take my own advice and attempt biography, as astute friends have long urged me to do. I suspect that a biographer has to have a greater variety of experience and talents than a novelist, that the different kind of imagination required is not inferior, and that in one sense no life has been lived and no event has happened until it has been scrutinized and recreated in art. However, the would-be biographer has to have the training and the judgment of a true scholar, a good deal of money for travel and research, a subject of keen interest to himself and probably to others, and important new material or a fresh insight from his own time, and preferably both. Skipping over my other deficiencies in this field, what has stopped me chiefly, so far, has been the lack of the right subject, approved by some publisher. I have flirted with a good many subjects for an article or a book, but always they have been overwritten, or already assigned, or supposed to be lacking in general interest. Living in Mexico, hoping to improve my Spanish out of a classroom, and being a democrat, I have naturally been fascinated by Benito Juárez. For all its faults, Roeder's life of Juárez is a little too recent and good for comfort. One way out seemed to be a short biography for young people, in a profitable series, but those publishers and others who might know assured me that very few Americans could be interested in Juárez. Well, Barkis is still willin', and looking around.

Twice, almost fortuitously, I have written books of essays. One, *R. F. D.*, on farm life at that time, for city folks, was accidentally successful, merely because a lot of people were thinking of going back to the farm, as we had done. Because most readers think I have written nothing else, I resent it a little and don't know whether it's any good or not. The other, *Wild Geese and How to Chase Them*, was cracker-barrel philosophy, unpopular and perhaps good. Having said farewell to fiction, and being still a wallflower in my long flirtation with biography, I have naturally thought again about essays, which are a special form of autobiography that does not demand an important or even interesting autobiographer to be good, and produced the present collection of essays. In this effort my first problem has been to write with pleasure, and to write well, with little hope of having the essays printed

and read. On this matter I refer back to a discussion above and add that, like many imaginative and lonely children, I invented playmates — in this case the six other members of an "essay club" who did not otherwise know each other but exchanged personal essays about once a month by mail. These were mostly professional men and women in different places, older and younger than myself, but mostly better read, more experienced, more intelligent, and more interesting than I am.

We come now to the fourth problem, that of doing well the job in hand. Clearly it is dangerous to discuss a medium in which you are offering examples of your own work. You cannot point out what seem to be your own little triumphs, and by revealing your standards, you indicate much more clearly the ways in which you have failed to meet them. However, a few remarks made strictly in general may not be too destructive. I do not need to be reminded that first excessive gentility and cuteness, and then information and argument, have almost destroyed the personal essay as a form. It is my hope that in an age in which poetry has become largely unintelligible and therefore arrogant soliloquy, there may be a vacuum into which the personal essay, with its precision of thought, feeling, and sensual evocation of moods, can return to acceptance and even be welcomed. The essay is also a letter, less personal than an actual one, but fresher if at the same time written with more care. If, as I say, the writer does not have to be important or even interesting, and if, as I would add, the merchandising of his personality is strictly taboo, his reveries, as distinct from the experience on which they are based, have to be strong, sensitive, highly distilled, expressed with amenity, an enchancement of living. A good personal essay delivers the inner content of actual life; it is reverie in a predicament, if only that of being alive; it is reverie enriched by memory and vitalized by danger and desire; it is reverie expressed with a candor, detachment, humor, and courtesy that are appropriate between unknown companions who would like to be purged of egotism in the presence of imminent death.

All of this clearly takes some doing, and when I read back through these essays on our present life in Mexico I am far from satisfied. For all its appearance of ease, gentility, and luck, this is a peculiar and brutal job, never done quite right. However, if by any chance you are thinking of trying to hire me away into some other, I may remark that the price will be very high.

13.   THE POOR MAN'S DILETTANTE

So it is that when I come up here to my little room to work alone I can soon become absorbed and happy, and remain so for hours, just as I can do when traveling alone, or in the best of company but often silent. Such hours, for which Hazlitt has recorded his relish, require some health and self-training, but are relatively an unearned gift of that selfless absorption in the "realm of essence" that many Orientals and other spiritual characters have considered the highest good possible in human life. In my own small, incompetent way I am inclined to agree with them; but I do not then think that desire, action, and society are intrinsically evil because they introduce the ego, with all its little hopes and fears, and thus tend to break down and corrupt that selfless absorption. The trick to be learned, the greater test of character, is not that of destroying the ego, but that of getting outside of it, in the midst of action and society, into contemplation of the whole situation or story, in which this ego is merely one little character with which we happen to be saddled. Unfortunately, because egotism and wickedness can often be fun, a good character is easier to handle in this way, in the long run, than a bad one, but I shall leave that side of the matter to the parsons and the uplifters. What I want to con-

sider, very briefly, is the utility and pleasure, in this effort, of
having an appropriate, well-fitted, and comfortable mask, or
persona, or part to play in public. This is especially necessary
for writers, retired people, temporary or permanent expatriates, and all the other attractive, somewhat nondescript bums
who will presumably be the most eager and best readers of
this little book.

We can assume at the outset, I hope, that we have all gone
beyond the elementary grades of living within ourselves, of
taking ourselves seriously, of wearing, in other words, rigid
and tragic masks that we never glance at and grin at in
mirrors. If we had not got beyond that kind of thing we'd
still be at home, holding desperately onto our jobs, making
good and getting all kinds of Recognition or slipping and
eating our hearts out, serving on committees, enduring and
harassing our families, giving our savings away, to the De-
serving only, spurning windfalls or worrying about them and
making a splash with them, and fetching up at home, not in
Mexico or anywhere else amusing, but in a much more
expensive psychiatric ward.

Why then, spurning and pitying all that, do we bums need
any masks, any roles, any parts to play in public at all? Can't
we be "ourselves," observers, free spirits, and nobodies, as
we are when alone? The fact is that as long as we have bodies,
clothing, shelters, appetites, the pack of always obsolescent
legal and commercial "papers" that society requires, friends,
neighbors, and these tiresome old characters of our own that
we can neither reform much nor exchange for new, as long
as we appear in company at all, we can't go without masks
without being dull, gelatinous oafs, any more than we can
go stark-naked without being banal and unattractive and
landing in jail.

A mask is one's response at the moment to the company
and situation in which he finds himself. Whether we like it
or not — and I like it very much — this world is a theater
in which the play lacks any evident author, script, or director:

we have to improvise as well as we can, and the characters
who die do not then rise, take a bow, clean up, change, and
go out to supper — except to "a certain convocation of
politic worms." We wear masks in order to identify and
express ourselves to ourselves and to our fellow players, and
this permits both them and us to act with more imagination,
authority, and style, and with a better production as a result.
Seeing it as a comedy rather than a tragedy, we change our
masks often, with the situation. As we age, if not before,
this constant changing of masks becomes tiresome, and we
look for a comic one that fits well but is still flexible and
expressive, and so can be worn more or less steadily. An
inappropriate mask, or a poor fit, is dangerous, because the
character beneath it tends to solidify in the shape of the
mask, or to tear it off with pain for all concerned. At middle
age or after, comical bums like us are apt to find ourselves
barefaced, if not actually bare-assed, and again pawing
thoughtfully through whatever wardrobe is available.

A man naturally tends to build his role, not too rigidly,
around his work or career, and a woman around her own
work or man, but these can vanish or prove unsuggestive for
theatrical development. Young hack in Greenwich Village
and Paris, schoolmaster in Connecticut, city-bred farmer in
Ohio, sailor in the LST's, pseudo-professor — all these roles,
with shadings and variations, and a few others, I have played
with zest, if with good or bad effect, but somehow, even when
successful as such, I have never been able to build up much of
a role out of my true work as a writer. Better writers than
I am seem to be equally unsuccessful. Hemingway is a He-
Man in Cuba or wherever, Faulkner the Old Confederate of
the Delta, Eliot the Literary Archbishop, and so on. Wander-
ing around absent-mindedly, listening and staring and brooding, and then spending hours smoking over a typewriter — it
just isn't good theater.

In Mexico the pressures towards a clear and forceful role
are slight. To the Mexicans I am just one more gringo, and

all I can do is try to surprise them a little, agreeably. Among the other gringos here in San Miguel I can be comfortable and effective as just one more aging misfit with just enough income to live here in the usual style and dabble in the fine arts. If I never went home I might not have given this matter another thought. In Chillicothe, Ohio, there is almost a tradition of non-functional eccentricity, and my ancestry and home would supply support for me if I cared to carry on this tradition, but there it needs definition and flavor, and in New York and New England it also needs force. Besides, some vein of theatricality or exhibitionism within myself, or some obscure hunger for precision and force, in behavior as well as in literary production, makes me dissatisfied with the fuzzy, unkempt, absent-minded, and disorganized idler that I observe in company and in a mirror. Every once in a while some unusually curious and candid person says to me, "What *are* you, anyway?" and I have to admit that I don't know. I don't lose any sleep over this question, but I was suddenly relieved and pleased recently when I thought of an answer: "Who? *Me?* Why, I'm a dilettante."

To be a good dilettante I shall have to know much more about many more things than I do now, but that could be an incentive. I am not a homosexual, but why should these so often arrogant unfortunates be allowed to dominate so many

attractive vocations and roles? I am not an elegant voluptuary,
but if I saw my new role clearly I might, as I did when I was a
naval officer, keep my hair cut and keep my pants from bag-
ging so grotesquely at the seat; and with Peggy as a teacher,
and with Maria to clean up the kitchen afterwards, I might
finally learn how to cook. Above all, I am not rich enough to
carry off this role with depth and style. However, my relative
poverty could be an asset, a limitation, like that of some
elaborate verse form, necessitating refinements and inventions.
The danger here, as with the rondeau and the villanelle,
could be a certain eventual thinness and tedium, but that
remains to be proved. One of the best dilettantes I know, a
maiden lady of eighty-nine, lives in her old home, in the
expensive U.S.A., on a shoestring. In books whom can we
find? Among those who have occurred to me so far, and then
been dismissed, because of either my incapacity or my distaste,
are Henri Beyle, Madame de Sévigné, Horace Walpole,
William Hazlitt, Walter Pater, Logan Pearsall Smith, and
Roger Fry. But there are many other possible models, and
in the end, of course, in this implausible and wonderful
theater with a single exit, everyone has to create his own role.

14. A LADY WITH A TROWEL

Sometimes these literary and personal questions, although
insistent and engrossing, can fill my head with smoke, just
as my cigarettes fill up my tiny room. When I stand up to
open a window I am apt to look down and see Peggy working
on her knees in her garden. Now there's something I'd much
rather ponder. Any human being, and especially a wife, is
a mystery not without its own special terror, but this one
usually has for me much more of delight.

Peggy is a woman in her fifties, a little over five feet tall,
rather plump — "dumpy," she calls it — with dark hair

streaked with gray and bobbed and waved; fresh skin, rosy
and tanned; an animated face with dark eyes behind shell-
rimmed glasses: altogether a rather tart and merry New
England lady, you might guess, and with some accuracy.
Almost none of her photographs satisfy anyone, and I'd like
to have a portrait of her for Oak Hill, but nowadays even
a pot of money would not be apt to get a good one. Titian,
Goya, and Rembrandt do not seem to be available, and very
few of the good living painters would be caught dead painting
a portrait at any price. If I can get her to sit still for a while
I am going to paint one of her myself someday, but that will
be like Rosencrantz and Guildenstern with Hamlet's pipe.

Peggy was born in Massachusetts, the daughter of a Unitarian minister of great charm, now dead, and his redoubtable
wife. Peggy has a brother and two sisters, all married, with
many children; two of these three have been divorced and
one remarried. The family life seems to have been violent
with love and tensions. For many years the family lived in
Baltimore. Peggy went to Bryn Mawr and was flunked out —
perhaps because she had poor eyesight and a quick mind
and was woefully inaccurate; perhaps because she had never
taken time to think. She went into professional Girl Scout
work and stayed in it successfully for many years, in Washington, Baltimore, Brookline, and elsewhere. When — as she
reports it — she finally decided honestly that she didn't care,
she dressed better and had plenty of admirers, chiefly platonic.
When she was thirty-four and I was thirty she had a strange
hunch that it would be a good idea to marry me, and I had
a strange hunch that that would be a good idea, too — for me,
at least.

Peggy enjoyed our eight years of farming very much, and
it probably would have been much better for her if I had
somehow managed to stay with it, even if I had had to give
up all notions of going to war or of writing. Someday, somehow, we may go back to farming in a small and unmechanical
way. During the war Peggy had a sister and various nieces

living and working with her at Oak Hill, and for six months she lived with her brother and his family near his naval station in California. During that time she had a bad attack of asthma and pneumonia, and she also worked in a bank. The banking system of California has not yet recovered full stability.

During our seven years of university life after the war, Peggy ran our apartment in Athens and every weekend we dashed home to Oak Hill and its garden. She got along admirably with my students, colleagues, and bosses, and she did more than her share directly for the university in planning the landscaping of some of the new buildings and in decorating the stage for commencements. That was another happy period for both of us, but the academic anemia and neuroses irritated Peggy more than they did me. Besides, she had married a writer, farmer, and sailor — not a hedging hedge-professor.

When my career took a nosedive and she had to leave her home, that was no fun, but her efficiency and good cheer were not merely loyal and dutiful: I think that she figured that somehow now I'd pull myself together and move forward. Having had some eccentric ancestors and a literary father, she did not assume that she should or could understand everything happening inside and to her husband.

If you spent a few weeks with us here or at Oak Hill you would of course notice many other things. At home or here in Mexico, Peggy keeps a clean, attractive house, full of flowers, without giving all of her time to it or being fussy about it. Every few weeks we are faced with a meal that is sensationally bad or skimpy, but usually we eat very well indeed. Peggy handles most of our financial affairs at home while I handle most of them in Mexico. Her desk is messier than mine, but she gets through much correspondence and paper work without serious confusions. She also makes some of her own clothing, and knits steadily for all of our friends having babies. As soon as she gets through her chores, her

first interest is in her garden, and she seems to be able to make almost anything grow almost anywhere. Another thing that she will always have to have, besides a garden, is a dog, and she spends a fair amount of time exercising, feeding, combing, brushing, delousing, defleaing, teaching, and playing with her four-footed pal. Naturally the results are apt to be good.

Each of us accuses the other of being entirely too gregarious, and probably both of us are right about that. We are not as much so as some of our friends, but we always have had a good many house guests and at least as many parties as we could afford. These friends and guests are most heterogeneous, and Peggy is equally good with an aging and ill musician or painter or some teen-age boy or girl, with a genteel parson or teacher or a much less respectable writer, sailor, or bum. She has a normal human interest in gossip without malice, but only once in a long while does she let her tongue wag dangerously. It doesn't often wag, but sometimes — quite without her intention or awareness — it does cut, and I attribute this to the astonishing roughness of the exchanges within her own well-bred family.

Also, having a quick, practical, and competent mind,

Peggy often knows better than other people what they should do, and how, when, and why they should do it. It is hard for her to remember that she does not always know, and that even when she does that is no excuse whatever for her *telling* them, for her assuming direction of a person or situation. Peggy hurts someone's feelings, or arouses resentment, every once in a while, but none but weak and humorless egocentrics have failed eventually to understand and forgive her, with a resultant deeper affection. This tart and bossy quality keeps some fools in their places while Peggy's old and dear friends can and do cheerfully and affectionately tell her off.

In content Peggy's mind is like a seachest packed full, in considerable disorder, of all kinds of rare, funny, and delightful things and a few items of unmitigated junk. Usually sitting up in bed and doing her nails, she reads very rapidly anything and everything from women's magazines and thrillers to very heavy tomes, usually quite beyond me, on archaelogy and architecture; everything from stage gossip and long, cheap historical romances to folklore and botanical history. She remembered, when I did not, the nickname of General George H. Thomas, "the Rock of Chickamauga," and I think she could tell you the names and present marital status of the sons of the Princess Royal of England, but I doubt if she could identify Thorstein Veblen or Aloys Senefelder.

Despite her ability to soak up all kinds of stuff with pleasure — "Oh, of course it's junk, and how I love it!" — her taste in reading is, within limits, shrewd and accurate, so that although she cannot begin to understand how any writer's mind works I have a healthy respect for her opinion of the results. In music her taste is as intuitive, faulty, and passionate as my own, and her ignorance is as great. In architecture and decoration her taste is better than mine, and better informed. In painting I had a long head start, and we are groping happily together. Once at a large luncheon I sat beside Peggy's mother while Peggy sat beside a museum director, and we overheard Peggy discussing Byzantine mo-

saics, or something equally esoteric, with this savant. "Did
you hear that, Allen?" asked Shenandoah, as I call her, with
a grin. "How much of it is secondhand nonsense?" "Not too
much, I think," I answered honestly.

One thing that, strangely to me, interests Peggy and every
member of her family is natural disasters: a great fire, flood,
epidemic, or earthquake is champagne and caviar to all of
them, as it is to the Mexicans. Of science, except practical
floriculture and intuitive veterinary medicine, Peggy knows
almost nothing, and her quick, assertive, medical diagnoses of
human ailments drive me frantic. In politics, thank God,
Peggy is a staunch and fairly well-informed liberal, and not
muddy-minded at all. I am so fervent in my gratitude because
I honestly think that in marriage basic agreement in politics
— as felt and practiced in daily life — is even more important
than agreement in religion.

Without being at all fussy or fanatical about it Peggy is
personally immaculate; however, she has a habit of filling
ashtrays with threads, bits of paper, wads of dog hair, pins,
peanut shells, and fruitstones; she hangs her numerous sewing
and marketing bags and baskets on any convenient door
handle; and she throws parts of any newspaper she is reading
all over the floor. She swims cleanly and expertly, if not now
very far, can whistle only out of the side of her mouth, in a
most remarkable manner, and has an unconscious trick,
when concentrating, of screwing one eye shut in a prolonged
and grotesque wink. Her laughter is frequent, gay, and honest,
especially over the telephone; some call it her giggle, which
is not quite the right word for it. In presiding over a meeting
or making a speech, she is oddly girlish and self-conscious —
at least, when I am present — and her New England accent
becomes much more marked.

Peggy cannot separate herself from physical pain and dis-
comfort: when she is ill, and only then, she wallows in self-
pity and thinks that nobody loves her or has the slightest
interest in giving her decent care. In the morning, when she

is well, she wakens rapidly and fully but likes to lie in bed
and plan her day and mine while I, in a somewhat resentful
daze, stagger up and try to get things started. It is a curious
and perhaps insignificant fact, which I have noticed in other
wives, that Peggy cannot really endure seeing her husband
asleep. She loves to soak herself in a tub, and in this house,
where we have so far only a shower, she misses this keenly.
Like most American women, Peggy worries a good deal about
her figure, weight, and diet, but she doesn't talk too much
about these matters, and actually her disposition is happier
when she weighs five or ten pounds more than she thinks she
should. She plays a very good game of bridge, I hear, and
although I can't play cards at all, she usually manages to find
three agreeable players for a regular game, which I call the
Hokinson Club.

One central fact is that although Peggy enjoys children,
and is admirably gay, kind, matter-of-fact, imaginative, and
firm with them, so that they naturally love her, and although
we have none ourselves, she has never to my knowledge
allowed this situation to distress her or make her neurotic.
This may be partly because we married relatively late, partly
because we have eleven nephews and nieces between us, and
partly because Peggy, like myself, has had several childless
aunts and uncles who were not at all neurotic about it and
were a great boon to a younger generation. Perhaps selfishly,
perhaps kindly, I have never particularly wanted children of
our own, or regretted not having them, but sometimes, after
reading some deep and turgid book of psychology, I have
wondered whether actually, without knowing it, Peggy has
not been cheated of "the full life of a woman," and so been
warped and stunted. Yet I have never been able to find any
faint trace of truth in this notion in her case.

I think that I could say much the same thing about her
lack of a career of her own. On the farm she was my full,
working, and happy partner; at the university she was almost
the same; and during the war she took care of herself and

our home sanely and admirably, while rushing off to any
seaport where I might appear. In every situation she finds
some kind of social work that she can do effectively without
display. Down here she sometimes complains that she doesn't
have enough to do, but when she goes swimming in the
middle of the morning, or stretches out on her bed, with a
book and her dog, in the middle of the afternoon, it doesn't
seem to bother her too much. Peggy has never devoted herself
to my career, and it would irritate me if she tried to. She
doesn't know enough about it, I'd rather handle it, with all
my errors, myself, and when women promote and manage
their husbands, it usually seems to me undignified and pathetic.
When I have made money, Peggy has enjoyed it and used
it well, and when I haven't, she has accepted that fact cheerfully and fatalistically. When I have received honors or been
hunted as a very miniature lion, Peggy has been gaily ironical.
As far as I can see, the only way in which my career has
really interested her has been in the only way I like and
need: when I write badly, she somehow smells it, and doesn't
like it; and when I write well, with my heart's blood, she
smells that, too, and then I sometimes see a fleeting, private
expression on her face that I rather enjoy.

But she didn't marry me and she hasn't stuck with me for
that, I am glad to know, because I don't do that often
enough. I couldn't begin to know why she *has* stuck it out so
long. I have, because usually she is such good fun, such good
company, on a lark, in a hard pinch, in almost any kind of
situation. To the young or romantic this may seem dismal
and limited. It is not so to me. During the Pacific war we
had a saying: "The kind of fellow you'd like to share a raft
with," and that's what I feel about Peggy.

I don't mean to imply for a moment that this marriage is
all "fun," in any sense of the word, for either of us. Once in
a while someone almost coos over "Allen & Peggy," and that
deserves a custard pie in the face. Like everyone else, we find
sex one of the most brutal farces, as well as one of the most

splendid wonders, that God invented. What frightens and
angers Peggy about me, and what would do the same to any
woman, is my lack of a kind of self-confidence, of concentrated
and persistent drive, of a good kind of egotism. I hope and
think this isn't exactly a lack of courage, because curiosity and
a certain amount of philosophical humor seem to see me
through the horrors well enough, but this thing is enough to
scare and infuriate any wife. On the other side, Peggy's
bossiness, which suggests some odd little lack of respect for
other people, some odd little insensitiveness to them, has not
much lessened in twenty-one years, and is not apt to do so.
Like most of her old friends, I can usually ignore it, or shrug it
off, or shout it down, but sometimes, slowly, almost insensibly,
suggestion by suggestion, intrusion by intrusion, it digs pretty
deeply under my skin. When I have been too weak and frantic,
or she too hard and bossy, or both have been so, too long,
we are apt to have a few perfectly ghastly scenes in strict
privacy. These scenes are costly, if necessary, and only partly
effective.

I suspect that for persons of any spirit, and of almost any
kind of weakness or stupid passion, marriage tends to grind
down, as well as to create, the finest personal relations, and
perhaps it does both almost at once. In any case, except
perhaps for the reasonable honesty and good manners that
we have to assume in each other in order to have time and
energy to do anything besides be married, nothing can be
taken for granted — nothing. The not quite impossible trick
may be to think about it objectively, to remember the good
things and imminent death, and to cultivate a sense of the
mystery, importance, and beauty of even the people we know
best.

That is one thing I have been trying to do here in writing
a little portrait of this woman who seems to me more delightful
and less difficult than any others I know, and like all the
others, unique. The mystery is there. I haven't the dimmest
notion what that woman down there on her knees in her

garden really lives for, penetrating all her pleasures and sustaining her through all her troubles, and I suspect that she hasn't any clearer notion herself. For those of us who are not truly or at least normally religious, the search for our deepest motives seems to be long, often unconscious, and perhaps ended only by death. Obviously Peggy would like to look like Mrs. Exeter in *Vogue,* produce an almost perfect garden, dogs, and household, be an unfailing help to her family and friends, leave whatever community she lives in a little better than she found it, and understand and help me without bossing. From my angle that's tops, and quite enough, thank you, but someday before we die we both may be able suddenly to see more in ourselves and in each other, and burst out laughing.

Meanwhile we may break up tomorrow, but on the whole, I think this unlikely.

15. A RAMBLE IN THE STREETS

The bank closes at one, and almost everything in town is shut down from that hour until four. Since we need a little cash and you want to see Dr. Olsina, we had better shove off now. Let's go on foot so that we can see more. "No, Jamie, sorry, not this time." Late afternoon is his hour, when it's cooler and we can give him a run in the French Park.

First we pass the two or three burros parked in our *callejón.* If we were taking the car, one of us would have to cast them off, lead them out of the way, and then return them. There on the chapel steps with his crutches, tipping his hat and greeting us politely, is Señor Rodriguez, the patriarch of the street. He has a fine singing voice in the chapel, and when his family and others put on in our street at Christmas the equivalent of a mystery play, he can write out the three-hour script from memory.

Don Carlos' little shop is crowded with country people and

with children, but his older sister has time to give us a cheerful
good morning. They say that she used to be called "La Reina
de Pulque," but that part of the business seems to have largely
dried up.

We go down the main street a couple of hundred yards and
turn into the neat little branch bank. The bankers have a
slightly chilly manner, as I suppose they do everywhere in
the world, with strangers, and the place is just as efficient as
it looks. We used to bank at Hoyos', a much more interesting,
informal, and humane little bank, where they also sell grain,
tires, eggs, dog food, and who knows what else. The Hoyos
brothers are so friendly and courteous, and we liked their
father so much, when he was alive, that we often regret our
defection in favor of more modern methods. Here in our
more modern bank there is one charming survival of other
times: an old beggarwoman hobbles in and gets a few centavos
from the cashier. He must have a box of coppers officially set
aside for that purpose.

Before going on, let's sit down for a while here on a bench
in the little garden opposite the bank, in front of the church
of San Francisco. The larger public garden, farther downtown,
in front of the Parroquia, might be called the big living room
of the town; then this little garden might be called the smaller,
more intimate one that the family likes better. There rises the
handsome Churrigueresque façade of the church, absorbing
in its fanciful detail and surmounted by a fine red neo-classic
bell tower. The large dome over the crossing, visible from
our *mirador*, and for miles around, cannot be seen here from
the garden right in front of the church. The trees give a little
spotty shade, and in the sunlight on the pool in the center
some ragged children are helping each other to stretch their
little bodies far enough across the water to drink from the
spigot. On the worn and broken benches perhaps a score of
people of all kinds are taking time out with us to soak in the
sunlight and speculate on the passing show.

Along comes, first, another very old and ragged woman

wrapped in the invariable dark shawl, or *rebozo,* bent almost double and extending a gnarled hand for some centavos, "for the love of God." As for us, we almost never give to begging children, but often do to these old women. How else can they live? And as I think Santayana has pointed out, they do not appeal to pity, or to the sense of justice, or to humanitarianism, but to something deeper that you can define more closely for yourself, if you care to. I suspect that life is dim in these old women, but not bitter.

Now two handsome adolescent boys, hatless, with hair oiled and slicked back, pushing their two bicycles, which are fantastically decorated with pin wheels and light reflectors. It is such young men, half educated, relatively poor, and feeling their nascent and frustrated powers, who join the political and religious fanatics of all colors, and who most dislike the gringos.

Now a fat and merry little *criada,* her hair braided and looped with bright blue or pink ribbons, a large basket on her arm, almost hurries to market. She will not hurry when she encounters her relations or girl friends, but her exchange of greetings with the cyclists is a bit cool. Perhaps working for Americans, she is probably doing all right as she is and doesn't need to take up with the first or thirty-first carousing and wife-beating young man who comes along.

Next, a family of three: a somber young countryman in ragged but clean white clothes, including the ancient apron around the loins and a huge old sombrero; beside him, a little to the rear, his tiny Indian wife, barefoot, with a large-eyed brown baby wrapped in her *rebozo* at her breast; the basic threesome, they have walked into town, many miles, from an adobe hut in the desert, and they glance at us briefly with the dignity of those who have their bare feet on rock bottom. What can we know or guess about them, or they about us? The hardest labor, animals, a little food, copulation, families, a furtive tenderness, a wild humor or rage, solitude in sunlight or darkness, death and the dark old gods always there — the

life in these people may be a small and murky flame, but it may be very hot.

Now a feeble and bent old gentleman, in seedy business clothes and felt hat, with a face that is a gentle but somber mask: that is Don Francisco Caballero y Frias, ninety-one years old. He has a dark little shop down the street, where he makes the *piñatas*, pots fantastically decorated with colored papers and filled with candies and fruits that children break at birthday parties; paper fire balloons for fiestas; dolls to be exploded in front of the Parroquia on the day of San Miguel Arcángel; *banderillas* to be stabbed into the withers of charging bulls; and who knows what other gay little fantasies to flower from the human tragedy he has watched so long.

Saluting Don Francisco respectfully, there goes our solemn, fat young banker in impeccable business clothes. He may well be only a generation or two from the adobe hut in the desert, but he has gone to school, and he can read, write, add up figures, initial checks with a flourish, and distrust everyone. If he is very careful he may someday sleep in a brass bed and be elected to the Lions Club.

Now a very tough-looking older man in a straw hat, a

kind of battle jacket, and short riding boots directs four or
five *campesinos,* wearing empty sacks over their heads and
backs, who are loading bags of cement on his truck. This
patrón may live in a huge, ruined, and very bare ranch house,
have a large bank account, and work very hard nonetheless.
He may be one of the few thousand men who, controlling the
one strong political party, the PRI, really rule Mexico. He
may do a good deal of strictly private worrying about various
members of his family. Perhaps one son is whoring a bit too
much after fancy wenches from Mexico. Perhaps a daughter
is a little too much under the thumb of the *padre.* Perhaps
the señora is rather tiresomely eager for an electric refrigerator. And all this while he himself doesn't know exactly how
long he can keep the whole show going if the rains don't come
soon for the corn.

And here comes a sensitive-looking young *padre* in a cas-
sock, black sack coat, black hat, and dark glasses — in our
town a safe compromise with the federal law that forbids
ecclesiastical costumes in the streets. He is accompanied by
a couple of clean lads in the blue pull-over sweaters of the
church school for boys. He jokes with them quietly, then
holds out his hand to be kissed by a countrywoman and her
three children.

Brushing by this group, two small but determined policemen, in elaborate but dirty blue uniforms, hustle a very big
and very drunk *campesino* off to the town jail, on the main
floor of the City Hall. The *cárcel* is not a place of comfort, and
we have already seen something of Mexican justice. This
poor drunk will probably be robbed by the police, he may
be out tomorrow, and he may be locked up for weeks.

Watching this scene with interest, there stands a tall, handsome American painter in blue jeans and a fancy shirt. Catch-
ing sight of us, he waves cheerily and comes over to explain that
the drunk is the favorite first cousin of his *criada:* by evening
she will come to her employer and try to borrow some money
to add to the family fund being collected to hire a lawyer.

That is all very well, the painter says, grinning wryly, but
damn it, he has a wife and four children of his own to support, and he hasn't sold a picture for months. He shrugs,
waves, and goes off with his empty tequila bottle to get it
filled with turpentine at the corner grocery store.

Notice that old man crossing the street so slowly. Bent
double, he is not more than four feet tall, and is almost
concealed, like the stem of a mushroom, beneath a huge,
shapeless, and very old sombrero. He is clothed in rags, including an old pair of my own pants that I think were once
at Okinawa, and over his shoulder he carries an old sack,
now almost empty. He is called Don Jesús de la Basura, Sir
Jesus of the Garbage, out of respect for his age, which is
over ninety. The garbage of the town is collected by truck,
but this service is so erratic that Don Jesús makes some kind
of a living by disposing of garbage privately. Watch: I will
give him a peso, as I sometimes do for luck, and if you can
manage to see the eyes beneath the raised hat you won't forget
them easily. To me, at least, they seem infinitely sad, indomit-
able, yet cunning. His ailment must be a painful case of
arthritis, and I don't see how the old man could hurt a flea,
but all of the *criadas* cordially dislike him and swear that he
used, at least, to beat his wife most cruelly.

Now there are a couple of American women trying to take
a photograph of Don Jesús. With a camera or two and a
light meter dangling from each neck, they certainly don't
lack equipment. Wait a minute: I, too, used to sneer snob-

bishly at these rich old American women tripping around
Mexico on the money that it killed their husbands to earn,
but there is more in these tourists than first strikes the eye.
I prefer them, for example, to those tough and glossy Mexicans
from the Distrito Federal, getting out of that big black car
across the street, with their pearls and their poodle, to inspect
the church. It is such people who are getting a dangerously
large share of the wealth of Mexico, and they think less of
their own countrymen, and do less for them, than those
American widows do. In the 147 years since Allende and
Hidalgo began to get rid of the Spaniards right here in San
Miguel, Mexico has replaced them with a plutocracy of
Mexicans much less functional than the *ranchero* we saw a
few minutes ago.

Now here come two other manless and aging women,
Mexican, and dressed in black. That big old war horse is the

directora of a large public school and, oddly enough, she looks remarkably like a distinguished dean of women I once knew in Ohio. This one doesn't like gringos, and is not exactly an appealing type, yet I fancy that if Mexico ever becomes largely literate and socially sound, women like this one, not men on horseback with rifles, will have done the job. But isn't her companion exquisite? She is a widow who owns and operates a little stationery store in which you can buy, among many other unlikely things, tinted post cards of sentimental lovers or of apelike wrestlers.

Now we had better walk down to Dr. Olsina's house. But here comes his friend and mine, of whom you have already heard something: Don Miguel Malo, often called affectionately Miguelito. He is a small, plump, and very active man, immaculate, with large, thick shell-rims and a face radiating intelligence, kindness, and wit. That greeting, so debonair if formal, was wholly sincere, and we Americans, as well as the poorer Mexicans, have hardly a better friend in town. No, he never speaks English although he probably could, and we rejoice in that fact, and in the care and pleasure with which he speaks Spanish slowly and precisely, for our benefit, gladly explaining anything that puzzles us. He is the only registered pharmacist in town, a high school teacher, and an antiquarian of knowledge and taste. His ancestry is distinguished, and he is proud of his family, while also very amusing at their expense. His childless wife is a religious recluse, daily he gives a great many free hypodermic injections to the poor, he has a house full of portraits and cats, and in a manner most un-Mexican, he gladly and skillfully does a little veterinary work on the side. Long before he made me that handsome and gracious offer, I had the warmest feelings of respect, affection, and gratitude for Don Miguel Malo.

Now here is Dr. Olsina's house. That shabby sign means that he is a graduate of the University of Barcelona, and is a physician, a surgeon, and an obstetrician. You remember that morning of the Schifrins' baby. Since that time he and Peggy and I have become better friends — even going as far as first names, second-person verbs, and *embrazos* — but Francisco Olsina y Boyer is not a man whom anyone knows well in a few weeks or months. His *criada* admits us, and we get a passing glimpse of his superior housekeeper, a daughter of his nurse. Under the doctor's knowing and exigent eye she can cook a splendid meal. We may have to wait here awhile in the passageway by the patio, because the doctor studies, talks, and plays cards at his club most of the night, and then, unless called out, sleeps until one. He practices medicine until late afternoon, and then teaches Spanish, Mexican history, and artistic anatomy at the Instituto, dining at nine in the evening.

The fine-looking little girl who spoke to us so courteously was his daughter. The doctor was divorced some years ago. This man has lived, and still does, although — probably in his late forties — he tends to harp a bit on his old age. In the Spanish Civil War he was a Loyalist, and landed in a concentration camp in France, where the medical experience, though not equipment, was extensive. Then I think he served with the Free French in Africa, and after the war escaped to South America, and finally to Mexico and San Miguel. His little daughter happens to be a citizen of Bolivia. Politically I should describe him now as a justly tired liberal. When he first came to San Miguel he did so much work free, and gave away so much medicine, that he nearly starved. He is still generous, if more careful, and with American clients and the Instituto job he seems to be doing better. Although still proudly Spanish and Catalan, he has entered into the life of the town, and no one could call him a *gachupín*. Here he is, a fine-featured little man, with long gray hair and shell-rims, in his dressing gown . . .

Yes, he is a charmer — isn't he? — as well as an excellent physician. I would trust him with anything except a serious operation — which he could handle himself all right but which would put Peggy or me into the nasty little town

hospital that he and others have long struggled to have replaced. So you two got into politics, history, and national
characteristics. It's lucky you weren't in there for two happy
hours, with another hour on art after that. I shall keep on
studying Mexico as long as I live here, and after that, and
Don Miguel and Dr. Olsina have helped me in this happy
effort more than any others.

— No, I'm afraid Mexico isn't that simple. However, let's
go into that some other time. By this time Peggy may be home
from her Biblioteca meeting, and we shall want a little drink
before dinner.

16. BOOKS FOR BENITO JUÁREZ

This "Biblioteca meeting" is held at noon almost every Wed-
nesday, and on those days we are lucky if we sit down to
dinner before two or half past. Sometimes I grumble, but
actually I am proud of Peggy's active part in this work, and
it eases my own social conscience vicariously.

As aliens, nominally Protestant, and a privileged minority
in San Miguel, we Americans, in this matter of social service,
as in others, have to be careful to know what our own business
is and to mind no other; but there are still things that we
can do appropriately and tactfully, and we do them. Although
she is an American, Señora Fernandez Martinez, as the wife
of the prominent Mexican owner of the Instituto, is in a
position to lead the almost continuous campaign for the
benefit of the *niños pobres* of San Miguel. With the help of
musicians who visit the Instituto, she and others such as Reva
Brooks raise money to give clothing to the poor children
every Christmas. The McFarlands, who are old Mexico hands,
and others, have raised a good deal of money for the new
hospital that this town may actually get sometime within
the next century. Already an X-ray machine has been given

by his friends in memory of Dr. Paul Bennett, a retired physician from Alliance, Ohio, who loved San Miguel and who was in his time the most gallant and cheering American in town. All of this is good, but it was more than a year after we came here this time before Peggy found herself a job.

Our friend Helen Wale is a divorcée and a grandmother, settled here apparently for life, who enchants most of the American men in San Miguel, including myself, and who is nevertheless admired and even liked by most of the women, including Peggy. Besides beauty, she has intelligence, taste, and a moral and social conscience verging on the quixotic. However, she also has an active sense of humor that she can and docs apply to herself.

Well, Helen Wale lives on a street near the center of town that may actually have more children on it per square inch than any other street in San Miguel. At almost any time of the day that street looks like a crowded playground during a school recess. When children kept coming to Helen's door to ask for American magazines to look at the pictures, she not only gave them to them, as we all do, but also invited the children into her house to use and share them there. Soon enough her house was almost uninhabitable, if full of good cheer, so she rented an old house next door, moved the children and magazines into that, and secured help from other American women to turn this happy enterprise into a regular library for children.

This Biblioteca Infantil has been active now for two years. It is open after school hours and on Saturdays, and the average

attendance is about forty-five children a day. Besides reading eight hundred or a thousand books voraciously, the children are given painting lessons, listen to stories, have movies loaned by the American and Canadian embassies, have parties, and have started a marionette theater. The employed librarian is a Mexican woman, a schoolteacher. Most of the books are in Spanish, but when friends in the book business in New York and in my mother's school on Long Island contributed more handsome and durable books in English, a committee translated them into Spanish and pasted the translations into the books. Once when I went to a Mexican lawyer to get my absentee ballot notarized I had to wait quite a while, cheerfully, because this lawyer was so busy translating one of the Babar books and laughing his head off.

During the first year and a half the receipts of this library, in cash, from contributions, dues, parties, lectures, house and garden tours for tourists, the sale of Christmas cards, raffles of contributed paintings and prints, and a reading production of *The Caine Mutiny Court-Martial,* amounted to $1717.68 U.S. During the same period the expenditures, for rent, light, the salaries of the librarian and two helpers, a training course for the librarian, renovations of the building, furniture, art materials, printing, entertaining, and purchased books, amounted to $1449.68 U.S. It is hoped that the Biblioteca can expand for the benefit of older children and adults, and eventually a house will have to be bought and rebuilt, so that more and more money will be needed.

The Biblioteca has its troubles, of course, but the women on the committee have been tactful, resourceful, and persistent, and have done remarkably little quarreling among themselves. Protestant or nationalistic propaganda has been rigorously excluded, so that when the senior priest of San Miguel made an accusation of this kind, one of his parishioners, the Mexican husband of one of the committeewomen, was easily able to refute it. This priest was invited to dedicate the Biblioteca, accepted, and himself selected the date. Scores of Americans and a good many Mexicans respectfully appeared for this ceremony only to learn that the priest had absented himself in Mexico City without leaving any word. However, this was ignored, a visitor from the States presented the Biblioteca with a mosaic of the Santísima Virgen de Guadalupe, and Helen Wale, when in Rome, bought a copy of the Sistine Madonna and managed to have it specially blessed for the Biblioteca by the Holy Father himself. This priest now openly supports the Biblioteca, for which we are glad. There have been some personnel problems, but so far, nothing insurmountable. Two of the American women on the committee are married to Mexicans and speak Spanish perfectly, while the others are learning steadily. Close contact has been maintained with the Benjamin Franklin Library in Mexico City. The organization of the Biblioteca has been very informal and fluid, but eventually it will be incorporated to assure continuity and to reassure donors.

It is impressive to me that for a few cents a day per child these American women are making available hundreds of good books, in attractive surroundings, to hundreds of poor Mexican children, and are in other ways opening up their horizons while taking scrupulous care never to oppose the interests and claims of their homes, their church, and their country. What thrills me most when I go into that cheerful house full of children groping for the great world beyond San Miguel is the very clear possibility that among these ragged little boys and girls there may be an Abraham Lincoln, a Madame Curie, an Einstein, a Benito Juárez, who might not otherwise find his way, and mankind's.

17. GLIMPSES INTO THE COUNTRY

Having farmed for eight years in Ohio, Peggy and I are naturally much interested in the ranches and ranch people

here, but these are very hard for foreigners to know. If it had
been a reasonable proposition, we'd have bought a small
ranch instead of this house in town; but the problems of
water and electricity, if any, would have been considerable
and, more serious, we should have had to keep at least one
whole family on the place all the time for security reasons.
Besides, this area, although on the eastern edge of the ir-
rigated "breadbasket of Mexico," is itself rocky and dry.

Every time we drive down to Manzanillo, on the west coast,
we pass through a region in the state of Colima, just above
the narrow coastal plain, that seems to have plenty of rain
and grass, complete with herds of cattle and cowhands. As
we drive through that country, I always think that if for
some reason we had had to come down here twenty or
thirty years ago I might somehow have got myself a cattle
ranch in Colima and experimented, when the idea came along,
with the Braham-Hereford and other new cattle crosses. There
is a story that some years ago Lázaro Cárdenas imported
some fine Hereford bulls, installed them on a ranch, and a
year or so later visited the place to check up on the bulls and

their calves. He was greeted with a big fiesta in his honor, at which was served barbecued beef — from the prize bulls. Nothing but the best for El Señor Presidente!

Speaking of Cárdenas, we are naturally interested in the redistribution of land, and in the *ejido* system of co-operative farms, but in this region at least we have found it hard to get clear and reliable information on this subject. My impression is that, with agriculture in Mexico being rapidly mechanized, wherever there is water the high cost of irrigation and of farm machinery and the exorbitant interest rates make small farms uneconomical — as we ourselves learned in Ohio, the hard way. If this is true it will raise again, perhaps acutely, the whole problem of land ownership. Right now it seems that the laws against large holdings of land are circumvented by putting small adjoining holdings in the names of different members of some large and rich family, who then quarrel among themselves.

The chief problem now is water, and the federal government is working on it valiantly. Mr. Michael W. Straus, former First Assistant Secretary of the Interior and United States Commissioner of Reclamation, who was down here last year visiting Helen Wale, told me that Mexico was spending a larger part of its budget on irrigation and hydroelectric development than any other major nation in the world, and that although the "leakage" of public money to private hands remained considerable, the results were nevertheless impressive, and would become more so. Recently the secretary of the Governor of this state, Guanajuato, told me that federal geologists had found plenty of water near San Miguel, and that the federal government was going to dig 150 wells for ranchers in this neighborhood. It sounds good, but Don Carlos, for example, has found that he will have to risk his ranch and neck to get wells dug on his ranch and then supplied with pumps and other equipment. Whenever and wherever the water is in adequate supply, I think the agronomic, economic, and political problems will be solved somehow in the interests of production, but whether any but the rich will then be better off remains another question.

One day a couple of years ago Peggy and I were invited, with some other Americans, to a "dinner in the fields," or *peek-neek,* at a large ranch near San Miguel operated, most unusually, by two handsome unmarried sisters in their late twenties. The ranch was owned by their father, an old and amiable man who went to sleep rather early in the day. Of this venerable rancher some very curious stories are told: that he was a potent revolutionary and anti-clerical who once in the twenties had sufficient political power to have the churches of San Miguel closed for a week for violations of the laws; that in his day he was one of the best horsemen and horse trainers in Mexico — and having ridden one of his horses, I can well believe it; and so forth.

The girls' brothers own and operate adjoining land, and are supposed to be among the toughest men in the region. Just recently some neighbor of theirs tried to kill one of them, but succeeded only in lodging a couple of bullets in a shoulder. These brothers don't like gringos, as their sisters do, and when a young American painter showed marked interest in these two girls, we wondered whether their brothers, or indeed the ultimately less favored one of the girls themselves, would kill him before he left town. Our impression is that these girls are not married because of their violent family, and because their modern interests and great abilities have got them out of one class but into no other. They have a town house in addition to the ranch buildings, which have not been much rebuilt since they were destroyed in the last revolution. On the ranch there is a village, and scores of people work for these girls, who supervise them mounted and armed. I suspect that they do as scientific and thorough a job of farming as can be done, and every year make or lose a good deal of money, depending chiefly on the rains.

That was quite a day. After eating, drinking, and talking hugely and well under a tree in front of the ruined hacienda, most of us went riding. Our hostesses were dressed in silk dresses, but sitting sideways in men's saddles, rode better than any other women I have seen riding anywhere — including those on a stag hunt in Somerset, England, in 1931. The younger one kept egging me on into races with her, which she always won, of course. We dashed up and down steep rocky hillsides that were thick with cactuses waiting to rip out our eyes, over water ditches, and across plowed fields. If those tough little horses hadn't been so beautifully trained, I'd have been scared stiff. On a last mad dash up to the ranch gates, where a score of ranch hands were watching this gringo critically, one of my reins parted, and stopped my horse too quickly, I went over his head and landed on a pile of rocks. I felt disgraced, but when I still held the horse and remounted him I had the great satisfaction of hearing one of the men say to another, "*Es un caballero, este Americano.*" I had not at that time mounted a horse for twenty years, so I paid gladly with a fortnight of misery. There is no fool like an old fool.

Unfortunately these remarkable women and Peggy and I have not seen much of each other since then, although we always chat a bit when we meet on the streets. There are just too many deep ravines of too many kinds between us, which even these wonderful Mexican horses cannot leap.

For two years now Juana, our former maid now employed by Helen Wale, has invited Helen and Peggy and me out to a small ranch owned by a cousin of hers to spend the day in celebration of this cousin's birthday. Unluckily both Peggy and Helen were out of town the first time, and Peggy was ill the second time, but I went both times, and shall keep on going as long as I am invited, simply because on that poor little ranch, in that good and generous company, I feel that I have come closer to the basic Mexico than perhaps anywhere else.

Juana is a pretty little thing, always cheerful, now a good cook, very religious, and quite irresponsible. When we hired her, she had at her breast a rickety and illegitimate small son,

a few months old, named Juan, whose life Dr. Olsina presently
saved, and who is now a fat and bouncing small boy. We also
became involved with Juana's father, who is an amiable
drunk, neurotic, and domestic tyrant; her all-enduring mother;
a sister with child whose husband had deserted her for the
army; another sister who married fairly well, for a wonder;
and two younger sisters, Cristina and Nicolasa, of whom we
became very fond and whom we helped a little into school.
Just recently we learned with alarm that Cristina, at thirteen,
had tired of school and got a job in Mexico City! If our
tenants had not fired all our help last summer, and if Helen
had not gallantly taken Juana on, we might have been involved with this interesting but tumultuous and exigent family
for life.

I say "gallantly" because by that time Juana, although still
unmarried, had again become pregnant. This baby was born
early, suddenly, and dead, one morning in a back room at
Helen's house. Somehow she and her *mozo*, Jesús, handled
everything until a midwife and Juana's mother and grandmother could be fetched. Juana's mother put the baby's body
in a shoe box, with flowers, had the death certified at the
City Hall, and had the little thing buried in the town cemetery,
without benefit of clergy. Within a few weeks Juana was as
strong and gay as ever, and had been readmitted to the lay
religious order from which she had been expelled. Even our
Maria had cast her off this time, but they are now friends
again. Whether Juana has learned anything much, I somehow
doubt. She and Jesús are very fond of each other, but unfortunately he is on the effeminate side. We think that she might
still get a good husband and make a good wife if her father
were not such an old devil and the whole family were less
demanding. This, then, is the background of those little birthday parties in the country.

At ten or eleven in the morning we all pile into our station
wagon, which has transported as many as twelve people, with
food and musical instruments. When we reach the ranch, only

a few miles out of town, there are at least a dozen more people already there. It is a dry farm of only a few acres, crowded down between the rocks and cactuses and the river. There is a very pretty, very small chapel on the place — almost a toy, made of marchpane — but this is always locked. The first year, the family had only one little adobe hut, windowless and thatched, but now they have two. They have two yokes of oxen, and pigs, turkeys, chickens, dogs, and cats wander here and there. We are greeted by the elderly parents and grandparents and what not of the birthday boy, who finally appears, very shyly and courteously, himself. I always give him one bottle of tequila — more would be dangerous within reach of Juana's father — and something else. Last time I chose, perhaps foolishly, a long, engraved knife, strictly for self-defense, because he and his partner had been attacked by some other men, seriously stabbed, and spent a week in the town hospital. In offering this, we made him pay a *cinco* for it, in accordance with our superstition about not cutting a friendship — of which, incidentally, they had never heard.

Now the musicians — three friends with guitar, fiddle, and horn — tune up, and Juana and Helen's Jesús, the best singers in the company, finally break into those wonderful sentimental songs. When we know any of the words, the rest of us join in. Modest amounts of liquor are served, made into a very good punch. All of us who can, sit on the little stools, and the children swarm shyly but affectionately over us. Meanwhile a turkey is being killed and cleaned, and most of the women are hard at work on dinner. Eventually this is served on long, low tables — an unusual luxury — in the dark little mud-floored huts. The first year, when she was working for me, Juana had furtively transported silver and a napkin for me, and I was seated at the head of the table and quietly given the best food. I was so embarrassed that I scolded her, and the next year, Helen and I were not fussed over so much, and scooped up our food with tortillas like the rest. The talk is always animated, but a bit difficult and confusing, and the only remark I remember is one of Juana's father's to the effect that *every* American is born with a talent for drawing and painting, and that *every* Mexican is an egotist.

After dinner we all wander down to a greensward beside the gleaming river, the music continues, the children and I go wading and skip stones, mothers nurse their babies, and anyone who wants to goes to sleep. The golden afternoon drifts away until finally we load as many of the townspeople as we can, including the musicians, into the station wagon and start back to San Miguel. The musicians play, and Juana and Jesús sing all the way, and so the old car with the Ohio license floats back into town on music.

18. HOMAGE TO HERMENEGILDO BUSTOS

It is not very often that we have the pleasure of watching the discovery by the art world, nearly fifty years after his death, of an artist of exceptional and indubitable merit. This case I enjoy especially because the artist was a Mexican who was born in 1832, more than three centuries after the Conquest, and who died in 1907, well before the "Mexican Renaissance" in painting. Add that Bustos was an extremely realistic if powerful imaginative portrait painter without training in Paris or anywhere else, that he probably never left his native state of Guanajuato, and that, although a patriot and a republican, he never painted a political cartoon on a wall, and this discovery, by Mexicans, acquires a very special flavor of its own.

The painting itself, of course, is the thing. Bustos painted a few religious pictures, but those that I have seen seem to me, although competent, melodramatic and not many steps above the thousands of bad canvases of that kind that were being painted at the time. Of his few sculptures, I have seen only one large crucifix, and while this is powerful and is relatively stylized and restrained, it would not in itself have caused any "discovery." Bustos also dabbled in architecture, but apparently without notable success. *The* work, the monument, consists of hundreds of small portraits, usually painted in oil on tin. Most of these are not more than a foot in the greatest dimension, and some of the best approach the miniature. The subjects are persons of all ages, mostly the artist's friends, neighbors, and relatives in the lower and middle classes in his home village, Purísima del Rincón, Guanajuato, near León, or in other towns in the same state. Collectively these portraits provide a fresh and moving vision of those people in that time and place, and also a deeply moving insight into the suffering, humorous, and powerful soul of Mexico itself, of the Mexico that bred Bustos and that will survive far beyond today. Painted with unsparing yet loving realism, these hard-bitten laborers and professional men, brooding mothers of families, and startled, ugly, dreaming children all have, in these portraits, the final dignity and mystery that only great artists can see and communicate, and that is rarely if ever fully felt out and delivered in any photograph. Technically, except in the use of some kind of gold paint for the jewelry, and in the introduction of sometimes lengthy and consciously humorous "legends," these portraits give no hint of the primitive. Bustos studied only a few months under an almost unknown painter in León, who made him a servant rather than a student, and it seems unlikely that he ever saw one painting by the master who inevitably comes to mind: Goya himself. Furthermore, there is little sign of any development. How this subtle, powerful, and only in the best sense highly sophisticated painting came suddenly from this uneducated village eccentric may be explained in time by his biographers and critics, but I doubt it. It is reported that Bustos usually did not need sittings, that his seeing his subject once, for a few minutes, was enough. Whatever the peculiar gift of the portrait painter who is also an artist, or vice versa, may be, this man was given it, magnificently, in his genes.

The personality of Hermenegildo Bustos seems to have
been so odd and charming that, in inevitably attracting attention, it may yet interfere with a just appreciation of his
work — "Oh, *that* character!" However, we'll take that slight
chance. Although Bustos persisted in calling himself an
amateur in painting, and never took students, he always
charged for his work — usually as little as two pesos a small
portrait — and seems to have earned most of his meager living
as a painter. A good part of his income probably came from
his *retablos* — those little pictures, painted on tin, of miraculous cures and rescues, featuring the divine intercessors and
the grateful human beings, that the latter still cause to be
painted and hung in churches. Bustos' *retablos* show more
skill and imagination than most, but are in the traditional
style. When painting failed to provide the beans and tortillas,
he did carpenter work and sold water ices in the streets —
often giving too many of these away to children.

He was married to Joaquina Rios, and they had no children.
"My little Joaquina has given me no family," he would say.
"However, I have my little Owl Bustos" — the pet owl that
followed him around his house. He also had a son by another
lady, Señora Santos Urquieta, and this son died young. On
the ceiling of a shop he painted a picture called Beauty Conquering Power, showing this lady — some claim, probably
in error — as Beauty in the act of paring the nails of a lion.

Bustos was a very devout man, went constantly to church,
and organized the religious fiestas in Purísima; he also liked
to discuss with friends such matters as the nature of the
Trinity. He played five musical instruments, and was also
keenly interested in astronomy, leaving painted records of
the comets and eclipses he had seen.

In dress, too, Bustos was distinctly himself. Sometimes he
wore with insouciance a most elaborate *charro* costume, but
more often the peculiar coat, designed by himself, that is
shown in his self-portrait, with his own name embroidered in
gold on the collar, and a number of embroidered crosses. ("I

painted myself on 19 June, 1891, to see if I could," he wrote on this portrait.) With this coat he often wore bright red trousers and a flatly conical hat in the Chinese style.

When he died at seventy-five, the whole village grieved, and there are people in Purísima today who remember him with personal pleasure as well as with pride. I think we can assume that Bustos had no notion of the quality of his work, and not the slightest interest in its future.

Apparently the first person to look at these portraits with appreciation was a writer of the same state, Don Francisco Orozco Muñoz, who collected them lovingly for many years. Somewhat later Dr. Don Pascual Aceves Barajas, of nearby San Francisco del Rincón, also collected Bustos portraits and finally turned his house into a Bustos museum. Meanwhile, of course, plenty of other people knew a good portrait when they saw one, no matter where. My friend Don Miguel Malo happened to see a portrait on a piece of tin that a woman was using as a dustpan, and she was happy to trade this old piece of tin for a new dustpan. Considering the thriving manufacture of "pre-Columbian" artifacts in Mexico, it seems to me likely that in a few years a liberal supply of "Bustos" portraits and *retablos* will be planted here and there in Guanajuato.

When Orozco Muñoz died in 1950, Bustos' work had become so well known that a *patronato*, or committee of patrons, was formed, and this committee purchased the collection and presented it to the nation. Señora Orozco Muñoz (born Dolly Van der Wee) had loyally refused to sell the collection, at greater profit to herself, to private collectors. The first Bustos show was held at the Museo Nacional de Artes Plasticas in 1951; but when I first saw some of the portraits, in 1953, and became an ardent *aficionado* — without, however, having the enterprise to begin at once to peer at dustpans — I found that many knowing Mexicans had not yet heard of Bustos. Some of Bustos' work has since been exhibited, as a part of the exposition of Mexican art, in Tokyo, London, Paris, and Stockholm.

It was during Holy Week, 1956, that Bustos' work first received truly national recognition. The state government of Guanajuato, in collaboration with the Instituto Nacional de Bellas Artes, and with the support of other institutions, of leading artists and intellectuals, such as Señor José Chavez Morado, and of nine embassies, held at that time the "First Week of Culture in Guanajuato," and dedicated this week primarily to the celebration of Hermenegildo Bustos. This fiesta was held in the state capital, Guanajuato, which is also the seat of the state university and is as cultivated as it is picturesque. Other features of the week were outdoor exhibitions and free movies put on by the embassies, lectures on art, a display of Guanajuato literature, symphony concerts, the ballet from Mexico City, and the continued outdoor production, in little plazas, by the University Theater of the *Entremeses Cervantinos* and the *Pasos* of Lope de Rueda. These last, directed by Lic. Enrique Ruelas E., have been running intermittently for four years, and have received international notice. However, the core and theme of the week was "Homage to Hermenegildo Bustos." This took the form of a comprehensive show, including the Orozco Muñoz (now national) and the Acevas Barajas collections, with additions and a scholarly illustrated catalogue; a lecture on Bustos by Dr. Aceves Barajas; and the dedication, in Purísima del Rincón, of a stone plaque to be placed on the painter's house.

This last was to me the most interesting and moving feature of the week. Twenty or thirty people, perhaps half of us foreigners from both sides of the Iron Curtain, led by the Governor, Dr. Don Jesús Rodriguez Gaona, and his staff, drove from Guanajuato to Purísima del Rincón, arriving about noon. This is a typical plateau village, except for the huge and magnificent trees in the public square. Bustos' house is also typical, a small adobe structure repaired with bricks, consisting of two rooms only, in front, and a yard in back with flowers in pots, nopal cactuses, and weary, cynical burros drowsing in the sun.

Mexicans are much prouder of their artists than we are of ours, and when anyone is honored, they feel that the entire community, with emphasis on the children and young people, should take part. The whole town was on holiday, a platform with awning had been built in front of the Bustos house, and the neighboring streets and the square were packed with bands, drum and bugle corps, school children in their gay uniforms, militia, the general public (half barefoot), and stray animals. The bands played well, school children sang lustily in a chorus, town officials and school principals made ringing speeches — patriotic, moral, cultural, and artistic — one of the school principals, a young woman, read a fervid poem by Dr. Aceves Barajas demanding that the name of the town be changed to Purísima de Bustos — an eventuality that is not at all unlikely — and the Governor received and dedicated the heavy stone plaque, which a workman had almost dropped on His Excellency's toe.

After the ceremony perhaps a hundred people, led by the Governor, crowded into the tiny vestry of the church called the Santuario, built by Father Ignacio Martinez, to inspect a large portrait of Father Martinez painted by his friend Bustos. Father Martinez, like Bustos, is venerated in Purísima, and the townsfolk had indicated strongly that they did not care to have this admirable portrait loaned to the exhibition in Guanajuato: if anyone wanted to see it, he could come to Purísima to do so. However, everyone was most hospitable, and several times natives of the town went out of their way to make sure that my wife and I saw and heard what we wanted to. Then in a cloud of dust, with the people of Purísima waving and saluting, with the bands playing, with the Governor's big black car in the lead, and with the Smart's battered station wagon bringing up the rear, we drove out of town.

In the shade of the great trees, in his embroidered coat, Chinese hat, and red trousers, with his little owl perched on his shoulder, there sat unseen the little figure of Hermenegildo Bustos, and on that tough but kindly face, with its big black mustache, there was an ironical but happy smile. It seems to me likely that within a few years the President of the Republic, art historians and critics from all over the world, and a lot of other people will find their way to Purísima. I can even imagine, less happily, the arrival of huge trucks, with many flashy people, to make a movie about the odd little painter, his wife, his owl, his mistress, the son who died young, and Father Martinez. In this movie an agent of Maximilian's will command Bustos to paint a portrait of the Emperor, and the painter, by this time a close friend of Benito Juárez's, will, with caustic eloquence and wit, and at the risk of his life, refuse even to glance at "this tinseled so-called Emperor, this pathetic tool of foreign power." Well, if this happens, there are worse people to "glorify" than good painters, and more *cincos* will thus find their way into the hands of the children of Purísima, for food — and water ices.

Meanwhile, someday, somehow, I am going to have one of those somber, stunning little portraits hanging on my wall before you do.

19. THE SUN AND THE SEA

On Sunday mornings we usually go down to the market, which is larger and more active on that day, with hundreds of people coming in from the ranches and with plenty of hucksters coming in from other towns to take their centavos away from them. Peggy always wants to see what odd new bits of pottery may have come in from Dolores Hidalgo, and what potted plants or cut flowers from Comonfort or elsewhere. San Pascual, who Maria tells me is the patron of gardeners, should certainly have received thanks from a number of old women with whom Peggy trades regularly.

After that we often drive several miles out into the country to a place called Toboada, where there are two small, open-air swimming pools fed by hot springs. This has been a very simple, unpretentious place, but now they are building a much larger pool, with restaurant, bar, and all the trimmings of a stylish resort. Meanwhile Toboada is ideal for soaking aches out of bones and muscles, getting a little tan, and chatting with friends. The smaller pool, round, is as hot as a very hot bath, and the larger one is only a little cooler, so that we can swim out there any day of the year. Some weekday mornings we play hooky and run off to Toboada, and to do

this in February, say, when we know that our friends at home
in the States are sloshing to work through slush and mud
under dirty gray skies, gives me a delicious feeling of luxury
and sin.

Much better, though, are the many noonday hours that we
have spent on the beach at Manzanillo, down on the tropical
west coast. Ever since we first went there by train, eight
years ago, we have called Manzanillo "Paradise, Mexico."
If the housing situation were better in Manzanillo, and the
summers down there less humid and oppressively hot than
they are supposed to be, we should probably be living there
today. In the days of Hawthorne and Irving, American writers
could get sinecures abroad from the government rather than
from private foundations, but even if I wrote a useful campaign biography of a winner I doubt that I could get the job
of American consul at Manzanillo. In the days of the Civil
War in Spain I publicly opposed Franco, which brands me
forever as a subversive character. Besides, the United States
has no consul at Manzanillo.

This is a little city of ramshackle huts tacked onto several
hills that surround closely a small harbor with a breakwater.
Big tankers and small tramp steamers use this harbor, there
is a small fleet of fishing vessels, and it is used as a base by
Mexican corvettes, frigates, and one inoperative small cruiser,
the *San Luis Potosi*. Naturally the population is more mixed
than in most places in Mexico, with a liberal condiment of
faces from the Orient and the islands of the Pacific.

Speaking of consuls, I once tried to rent a house from a
Mexican businessman in Manzanillo who turned out to be
perhaps the most active consul in town, representing several
governments in fact, but officially only that of Denmark, with
photographs of the Danish King and Queen in crowned frames
on his office walls. This reminded me happily of one of the
most remarkable men I have ever known: the Danish sailor,
novelist, and art critic, Kaj Klitgaard. Manzanillo is like that:
recalling and suggesting all kinds of things.

The Mexican Navy, for example, always fascinates me. To Leonard Brooks (Lt., R.C.N.V.R.) and to me it seems weirdly unmilitary, but in its function as coast guard it may do a good job, for all that. The officers are usually immaculate, and the enlisted men very dirty. I once made an appointment to go aboard one of the corvettes moored at a pier, but when the time came, some special inspection banned all visitors. Once a half dozen of the little ships held maneuvers within sight of the beach, and I must say that even our LST's, which were notorious for some things, if famous for others, could have given those boys a few pointers. The midshipmen, in faultless whites, wear little swords, with white gloves hanging from the hilts. At Christmas time each vessel has a decorated Christmas tree — a thoroughly un-Latin custom now becoming very popular in Mexico — secured at the top of the mast.

Because of the lack of room on those steep hills, between the harbor and a large lagoon, the town is very crowded, many of the streets are stairways, and the houses — a mixture of modern concrete buildings and thatched matchboxes — seem to be fastened to their perches with baling wire and chewing gum. At the fiesta of the Santísima Virgen de Guadalupe, in December, and on through Christmas, and doubtless in other seasons when we have not been there, nearly every house is decorated with colored paper streamers and with Japanese lanterns. Seen from the beach across the harbor where we always stay, when the sun goes down in gaudy splendor into the Pacific, the stars appear, and the lights come on in the town, with the mountains looming darkly above it, the whole show is blatantly and almost comically romantic to an extreme.

There is a manganese mine up the coast, and a banker told me that huge deposits of iron ore and limestone in the neighborhood will result in the building of iron and steel mills, so that in time, he said, Manzanillo will rival Monterrey as an industrial city. This is a possible future to which the banker naturally looked forward more happily than I could.

Meanwhile the whole region is as beautiful and interesting as the town. For the most part, the surrounding mountains go right down into the sea and the long Pacific swells break on rocky cliffs, but in between these there are great arcs of clean, sandy beach, backed by palm groves and jungles, with thatched villages tucked in odd corners. The bird life is not so spectacular as it is, for example, at San Blas, farther north, in the state of Nayarit, but it would still delight and satisfy anyone but a perfect glutton for birds.

One of our best trips in the neighborhood was when Peggy, Jamie, and I took a bus to Barre de Navidad, up the coast, by way of Cihuatlán. Barre de Navidad itself was a wretched little dump of a village on another beautiful little harbor, something like that of Manzanillo, although even smaller. What made our trip was the fact that the river at Cihuatlán was running high, and a ford being built had not been completed, so that the bus stopped at the bank, we were ferried across in skiffs, and we then caught another bus on the other side. When we returned in the afternoon we got back across the river only to find that the bus waiting there was going to stay just where it was for another four hours. Meanwhile the traffic across the river, of coconuts, bananas, cement, people, animals, etc., continued very active. Every now and then a truck or even a passenger car would rashly attempt the crossing, get bogged down, and be hauled out by a man with a large tractor and high prices, waiting there for that purpose. The bargaining was stiff, and the general laughter was uproarious. Meanwhile people were wading across, and some went swimming for pleasure, or accidentally. Every now and then two or three mounted cowhands would appear with a herd of cattle and drive them across, with the younger calves struggling valiantly and their mothers encouraging them. The scene was so animated and happy that the four hours passed very quickly.

During this time all of us waiting for the bus to start had

become very friendly. I made a sketch of the scene and gave it to a fat old woman with whom Peggy had been chatting. As usual in such cases, she sincerely tried to pay for it. It appeared that she was the sister of an even fatter and very dirty priest who was the congenial senior member of the party. A man appeared with some buns that some of us bought and all shared. After a while one person after another had to withdraw to the bushes, and there was much joking about paper borrowed for this purpose. As usual in remote places, Jamie attracted much curiosity and admiration, so we made him do all of his tricks in the aisle of the bus, and he then received what amounted to an ovation. One woman politely asked Peggy whether she could borrow her glasses to read a letter from her son that she had been carrying all day. Peggy's glasses are strong and unusual, but they seemed to serve very well. The road back to Manzanillo, in the dusk and then thick darkness, had appalling holes in it from floods, big enough to swallow the whole bus, but the driver drove very carefully.

Next to those spent in painting, my happiest hours at Manzanillo have been those that we have spent merely lying on the beach. We usually stay at a good little motel, although once two very nice women loaned us their cottage nearby for a fortnight. These places are only a few yards from the water, the surf is not too heavy there, and the beach slopes so steeply that with only a leap or two first one can dive in.

To soak in the sunlight on the sand, watching the waves, the sand crabs, the occasional beachcomber passing by, and a ship entering or leaving the harbor; to listen to the surf and the wind in the palms; to sense Peggy near me, happy now in her handsome body; and to feel the sunlight, the air, and the sea reaching into, relaxing, and cleansing every dark, tight corner of my own mind and body — this does very well, thank you. Finally we go in for a drink, a good dinner of sea food, and a nap.

All of this is the kind of thing that some of us dreamed of during the war, when we were exhausted mentally and physically, tortured by the constant drive and the steel grip of discipline, and so far from our women, our homes, and liberty that we truly doubted their existence, and in such a world were not too much alarmed by the possibility that that night a bomb could splash our brains and entrails against the bulkheads. A stranger thing that I dreamed of then but have not attained is harder to explain clearly, without shyness. Let us say I hoped that if I lived through that I could somehow, before I died, clean my mind of violence and egotism and everything shoddy. I never shall, but the sea and the sun do help.

20. THE ENVELOPE OF POISONED AIR

We get most of our mail in a box at the post office, and usually sit down to read it, with a drink, in the breezeway or on the terrace just before dinner.

The interruptions are constant, because it is at this time of the day that most of the people who have or want to have business with us come to the front door. There is the little old woman with tortillas for Maria and Jamie. There is another little old woman with one egg, minutes old, in her gnarled hand that she wants to exchange at once for a *tostón*.

There is the voluble and theatrical strawberry man. There are a couple of ragged *campesinos* with burroloads of wood that Maria laughs to scorn. Here comes one of the ladies from the Biblioteca committee to discuss the latest problem with Peggy. It was at this time that my friend, the writer, Mick McComas, used often to drop in, as another writer friend, Norm Schmidt (James Norman) does now, so that we can happily reinforce each other's information and prejudices about Mexican and American life, politics, and history. Mick had to return to California, and most painters don't know or care much about such things.

In any case, with the arrival of the huge Sunday New York *Times* on the following Thursday or Friday the whole world floods into our little ivory tower. One fairly common view on this matter is that since most of the news is so alarming and depressing, since we cannot do anything about it, and since we *have* found ivory towers, for the time being, however shaky their foundations, the sensible thing to do is simply not to read the news. This view I cannot share, partly because I think it's a sacrilege not to vote as intelligently and regularly as possible, partly because keeping reasonably informed may help me to escape that rootless, floating, vaguely neurotic character that can be detected in even the more charming and mentally stable of expatriates, and partly because I'm just plain curious. When we go back to Ohio to live, I may look like a Rip van Winkle, but I don't want to feel like one.

In 1956 we were swept back into the world. Illnesses in our families, business and legal affairs, and medical check-ups kept us in Ohio, New York, and New England for five months. Over TV — which, nevertheless, we are quite happy without — we stared bug-eyed at the political conventions, the all-Australian finals in men's singles' tennis, an enthralling World's Series, and most of the major speeches of the campaign. We also did a little quiet politicking, handing out on the street corners of our home town sample ballots marked for Democrats. We are unreconstructed Northern, New Deal-Fair Deal Democrats, and were strong for Stevenson, so that many of our more plush friends think that the poor Smarts have a slight touch of leprosy. Then came the explosions in the Near East and Hungary. After four years of blind bungling and bad faith (as I see it) by Dulles, strongly supported by Eisenhower, our allies ditched us and knifed the UN, and our whole foreign policy collapsed. (It seems to me quite possible, as it does to the best economic brain I know, that our fantastic economy will do the same, or that dollars will become the smallest change, or both.) Yet a few days later our fellow citizens swept their moralizing hero and his gang back into power. Unlike most Republicans I know, I consider it a possibility that I may be wrong and my political opponents, especially when they are in a large majority, right. However, I was glad to return for a while to Mexico, where it is easier to dodge the news.

With the language difficulty and others, it is hard to find out what Mexicans honestly think and feel about the United States and the world situation, but I have picked up a few hints — which you can discount as you see fit, because of my own political position. Our intervention in Guatemala — and it was that, whether necessary or not — was strongly opposed by many thinking Mexicans. Informed persons have told me that our present Ambassador "knows and cares almost nothing about the Mexican people," and that he "even entertains the absurd and dangerous illusion that the Mexicans can be persuaded to give us back their oil wells." Before learning my own political prejudices, many Mexicans have told me that whatever aid we now give them or loan them is now rigged for the benefit of our large corporations and — perhaps not quite inadvertently — of Mexican plutocrats, and that, except for these, most Mexicans remember longingly the Good Neighbor policy and the attitude it expressed.

My impression is that Mexican friendship for the United States is diminishing daily, and that what remains is fed by tourist money, by less sordid personal relations, and by the anti-communism of the Church and of most Mexicans. They feel small gratitude for the shield of our military power, simply because of the danger to Mexico, and to civilization, of our new weapons, as well as the Russians'. Of course the ordinary ignorant or semi-ignorant Mexican in San Miguel is not much aware of or excited about the possible destruction of most of the world's great cities, but the educated people of all political colors feel this chill in their own entrails. On recent events these people clearly supported our position in the UN, and any other would have proved to them our colonialism. As Don Carlos put it to me rather magniloquently, "The paladin of the West was betrayed by her European allies." However, most Mexicans, I am sure, would sneer at this startling new phrase for the old "colossus of the North." More typical is a remark made to me by a relatively well-educated Mexican whom I hardly know one sunny noon in the *jardin* while I was reading a Mexican newspaper.

"Señor," he asked me, "why do you bother to read our newspapers? The history of Mexico is being written in Washington."

I am never quick and effective in answering such a sudden and interesting question, and I cannot remember what we said, but the dialogue might have gone on like this:

"Hardly more, señor, I think, than in Moscow, or in Mexico City, for that matter, or in any one of sixty capitals. Our histories are even being written a little, thanks to God, in the United Nations."

"I have little faith, señor, in institutions as such. They can only express, they cannot improve, human beings. Lethal and suicidal as all nations now are, a more effective federation could easily become a world tyranny, and worse than armed nations afraid of world opinion."

"They are not enough afraid of it, and could be made more so. I am sure that most people everywhere are now good enough and strong enough to get a safer, better world. I am

sure that most people everywhere want peace, justice, and liberty; want them for themselves, and for their own safety, for others everywhere, and even at their own risk and expense."

"You are very optimistic, señor."

"Perhaps, but I have been called that before, and I should say that I merely want to live a little longer, and have an odd interest in seeing the human race do the same. Put it this way: as a patriotic American I should have been glad if world-wide opinion had been truly expressed, not only on Hungary and on the seizure of the Suez Canal, but also on the creation of Israel, on the bomb tests, and even on the destruction of Hiroshima and Nagasaki — which, incidentally, may have saved my own life."

"Do you imagine that the rulers, or indeed the people who voted for them or tolerated them, would have paid much attention, or would now do so? Your Mr. Stevenson, for example, was badly defeated, the British are screaming for their lost prestige, and I can imagine the laughter over the vodka in the Kremlin."

"The rulers and the people have already shown fear of world opinion, which has not yet been fully discovered and expressed on anything. This interests me more now than

any more artificial and dangerous strengthening of the United
Nations. That is one reason why — besides the good art
criticisms — I am now reading your newspapers."

"As a writer, señor — for I have been told that you are
one — have you done anything about this, or do you propose
to do anything?"

"Fair enough, señor! The fact is that I have had no training
or experience as a newspaperman, or as a pollster, and that
readers prefer my little pieces on dogs or landscapes or
painters. I may do something about it someday. Meanwhile,
while I can, I am going home to dinner."

21. THE TIME OF TROUBLES

In the middle or late afternoon we go down to the Instituto
Allende for lessons in Spanish and art. Nowadays the Instituto
is an art school that has responsible owners and is housed in
a magnificently rebuilt hacienda on the edge of town, with
a new hotel attached. I sometimes wonder how many of the
boys and girls and aging people who work and play in those
studios and sunny patios know or care anything about the
school's "time of troubles" eight years ago. Those of us who
lived through that time found it highly educational — if in
politics rather than art.

In an odd manner that I shall explain elsewhere, Peggy
and I got six months' leave from my job in Ohio and came
down here as students dependent on the GI money. Peggy
plunged happily into housekeeping, weaving, and photography, and I into painting. Within three weeks came the
explosion.

The school was owned by a lawyer named Campanella,
who had bought it accidentally as a part of a ranch, and who
knew and cared nothing about art. However, he quickly
found a way to enrich himself with GI tuition and materials

payments while paying out almost nothing for equipment or
in salaries to his Mexican, American, and Canadian teachers.
In the old monastery that was used by the school, David Alfaro
Siqueiros, the soldier of fortune, painter, Communist, and
would-have-been assassin of Trotsky, had begun to paint a
truly original mural, with only republican content, on the
life of Ignacio Allende. Because of its technique this was
attracting so much attention that Campanella urged him not
to finish it too quickly, and offered him a contract of some
kind that he found insulting. Siqueiros withdrew and, securing
the support of most of the important Mexican artists and
intellectuals of all political colors, published in all the newspapers a violent, full-page manifesto "exposing" Campanella
and "boycotting" the school. Because they had been exploited,
and because they could not afford and did not wish to take
sides against artistic Mexico, the American director, Sterling
Dickinson, and all the teachers resigned in a body. Because
we could not support Campanella against all these, our
friends, and because no classes were held anyway, most of
us hundred-odd students walked out on the owner also. Immediately and naturally the Veterans Administrator at the
Embassy, who had hitherto shown no interest in the school
whatever, stopped all payments. Dickinson, the teachers, and
we students promptly secured another building, cleaned and
painted it, went to work in regular classes more vigorously
than before, and applied to the Mexican Government for
recognition as a good school. All of this was a preliminary
to applying to the VA for reinstatement.

There were probably half a dozen Communists among
the students, but of course only the most sincere and least
active one of them admitted it, and Siqueiros kept claiming
that his protest was cultural and not political. With hindsight
only, it is easy to point out that Dickinson might have dis-
sociated us from Siqueiros and his little stooges and associated
us more effectively with the VA Administrator. However,
it should be noted that this VA man was, to say the least,

confused and incompetent himself, and may well have had his orders from Washington.

There was now naturally some delay as well as general anxiety, and bad things began to happen. Most of the students and their wives were good people, studying seriously and behaving themselves, but a *Life* article on this "G.I. Paradise," with a photograph of a nude model, had resulted in a flood of applications for admission, and despite precautions a narrow lunatic fringe had inevitably got in. One night one of the nuts, in a fit of jealousy, bashed in the head of another with a portable radio, and so killed him. Not long after, the killer quietly escaped to the United States, probably to the great relief of the local authorities. The senior priest of the town, who holds that office to this day, denounced all Americans as Communists, and urged their servants to leave them. This was ignored by the servants and repudiated by the city administration, and one rumor was that his bishop had reprimanded this priest. The Lions Club and other Mexican groups came strongly to our support, and when we marched in a body in the parade on the national holiday, we were pelted with flowers. At about the same time, however, some young men, religious fanatics, placed a homemade bomb in a front window of a house belonging to Colonel Johnson, a retired American Army officer on our side, and blew up his fortunately empty sala. Meanwhile most of us were wondering how long we could hang on in San Miguel without GI money, and many were going home.

Siqueiros may have felt some of his responsibility for all this trouble and hardship, or perhaps he saw another chance to publicize himself. In any case, he organized an attempt to spur the Mexican Government by presenting a petition for the recognition of the school to President Miguel Alemán himself. This was to be presented personally by Siqueiros, the elected head of the student body, and a teacher, Leonard Brooks, at the grand opening of the fifty-year retrospective exhibition of the works of Diego Rivera at the Palacio de

Bellas Artes. Most of us stayed at a sordid little hotel in Mexico and conferred with Siqueiros at a coffeehouse. Although skeptical and nervous, like all the others, I helped with the wording of the English translation of the petition, which was printed in both languages.

When the big night came, each of us took a packet of the leaflets under his coat, and we proceeded to the Palacio in a high state of nerves and a low state of dysentery. There was a huge crowd of all kinds of people, and I remember handing leaflets to ladies in diamonds, to barefoot Indians, and to some of the armed guards who came in with the President, before dumping the rest under a statue of a nude. Siqueiros and the two others made their way safely to the President and Rivera, and formally presented the petition to the former. It was graciously received, and within a few days, to our surprise, the Minister of Education sent careful inspectors to the school, which was quickly approved.

Now our future was in the hands of the VA man, who was more important to us than the President of Mexico. My theory is that he was annoyed, frightened, and eager to get rid of a mess for which he was clearly in part responsible. In any case, he took care to delay reinstatement of the school until a date had passed after which, a new American law decreed, no new school could be recognized for GI payments. Then he claimed that, although the director, faculty, and

students were the same, the school was a new one, and could never be recognized by the VA. We now had another petition printed and mailed it to all our congressmen and senators, to the VA head in Washington, and to the President of the United States. Probably because Sequeiros was a Communist, and a VA blunder had to be forgotten, this petition was firmly ignored. Several scores of good American veterans, with their wives and children, packed up, borrowed a little money, and went home. With help from home Peggy and I managed to remain until our leave was up.

Months later there was a nasty final chapter. Campanella was going broke, and was vindictive. The "new school" was still operating in a small way, the teachers who had defied him were still living happily in San Miguel, and he couldn't stand it. He had already broadcast among colleges in the United States a lying attack on Dickinson. He now bribed some minor Mexican immigration officials, and as a result one day armed officers appeared at the homes of all non-Mexican teachers, forced them almost at once aboard a train, and escorted them to Laredo. They had very little money. They were separated in some cases from their wives, and in all cases from their homes and possessions. From Laredo they telegraphed to Siqueiros, who made some ineffective noise in Mexico, but what actually rescued them was a telegram from Brooks to the powerful General Beteta, to whom he had given water-color lessons. Under General Beteta's pressure high officials retracted the action and readmitted the whole group with new and better papers.

Campanella left San Miguel under a cloud of bad debts. Retaining Dickinson as director, Don Enrique Fernandez Martinez, an ex-Governor of Guanajuato, and Dr. Felipe Cassío del Pomar, a Peruvian and the original owner of the school, took it over and installed it in its present handsome building. Don Enrique later bought out Dr. Pomar. The rest of us, the GI's who were in the middle of this mess, have our memories, our slightly advanced political education, and pre-

sumably augmented, "unevaluated," and secret dossiers in
the files of the FBI. Well, a lot of other good people have
much the same, and in our case the education may have been
well worth the slight hardship.

22. A PRIVATE COLLECTION

Peggy has a few fine pieces of old glass, and here and at home
we have a small collection of drawings, prints, and water
colors that we hope slowly to increase and refine, but in the
ordinary ways neither of us has the instinct or the money of
the true collector. However, all my life I have indulged happily and more or less privately, as one must, in a very inex-
pensive form of collecting that I find profoundly interesting
and satisfying, if sometimes frustrating. I collect memories
of people.

Sometimes I write little portrait sketches that get into books,
and this I enjoy, but the writing is not essential. When I
worked for that great collector of American lithographs, Mr.
Harry T. Peters, he used to advise other collectors to limit
themselves, to specialize, but in collecting people, I am not
sure that this is advisable, and I am sure that any kind of
rigid classification is falsifying, because every specimen is
unique, and the differences are more interesting than the
similarities. Classifications of people, such as Jung's, or
Hinkle's, can be enlightening, but when you look at any given
specimen carefully, these tools finally fall away. It may be
useful to consider Doakes as a painter, as a "sensing-intuiting
introvert" or what not, as a sexual or civic specimen, and so
on, but what is exciting in the end is his essential and unique
Doakesism. If this is remembered, a tentative grouping of a
type is harmless enough, and right now I want to leaf through
a few people who have this in common that always delights
me: they are all people whom it would be easy to misjudge.

For my part, I can never quite make up my mind about the relation between physical appearance and character. It is clear that glandular and other physical disturbances and peculiarities affect both body and mind, and we have all seen, in adults, how character and the experience it has brought can subtly ruin or transfigure faces, hands, gestures, and the carriage of the body. In the other direction, a body that is unusually large or small, beautiful or ugly, or what not, from conception, can clearly affect character and destiny. If we did not have this common fund of experience and judgment, there would be no room for the portrait painter, honest or dishonest, the storyteller would lack one of his most important if tricky tools, and detective services and credit bureaus would have to be much larger. However, among the women I have known, one of the purest spirits looks like a very sultry tart, and one of the kindest and most scrupulous must surely be mistaken quite often by strangers for a transatlantic cardsharp. Among the men I have known, one of the most kind and sensitive, although thoroughly masculine, looks at first glance very much like a gangster. My own mother is an able and impressive-looking school administrator; if you saw her walking down an aisle with others in her academic robe, I doubt that you would guess that an hour later, in the right company, she could mimic herself and the others in that procession with wicked and wonderful wit.

If firmly regarded as specimens only, another class, hypo-

crites, can be a great joy. We have all known a charming
clergyman or two who wormed his way into the affections
and sometimes the beds and bank accounts of some of his
more pretty and feeble-minded female parishioners. The type
is *muy corriente,* but still amusing. Once on Long Island I
knew a character who seemed at first common enough, but
kept growing into his own kind of real beauty. He was a
"pukka sahib" or "professional gentleman." He never failed
to bring finally and gently into the conversation his distinguished family, his noted friends and acquaintances, his own
impeccable taste, and — when a little drunk — his exploits
and decorations as an army officer. Any collector would have
surmised quickly some concealed flaw in this handsome
picture, some bitter humiliation that forced this self-portrait-
ure. Nor was it any great surprise when I discovered that
although very well married — such characters often do get
attractive and valuable women when young — the Major had
made a pass at every woman in the community under eighty
without a squint or a club foot and with more than five
hundred dollars in the bank. Then after a married woman
we knew had been unlucky, or at most indiscreet, the Major
climbed on a very high moral horse and went galloping all
over the place denouncing her. I had not suspected that his
own philanderings had troubled him so much, or else that
he himself had hankered for the woman in question without
the dimmest chance of ever getting to first base. The final
touch will surprise only the beginner: when the Major's wife
slowly and deceptively, in the most ugly and painful manner,
lost her mind, his behavior, very quietly and privately, was
heroic. I still went to some trouble to avoid this man, but
he moved into an upper drawer of my collection.

Professional hypocrites are rarer, and in a way more
charming. Once on the Dover train from London, my classmate and old friend, Tony Glick, and I had the great good
luck of seeing at work three professionals. One might have
been a retired butcher, another a seedy clerk, and the third,

the leader, a music hall entertainer long out of work. Naturally they gave no slightest sign of knowing each other. The third began to play, with cards, a variant of the shell game, and put on a truly subtle and effective pretense of simple good nature and cowardice. The butcher won liberally, and the clerk tried to get Tony and me to play. Having had no success with us or with the other travelers in the compartment, the three of them detrained suddenly at Canterbury. At Dover I reported them to a policeman, who questioned me carefully and then told me that the "entertainer" was "Little Tich," nicknamed afer a famous music hall comedian. He and one of the others had been released from Dartmoor a fortnight before, and the police had been alerted to watch for them on the boat trains. This was their first reported appearance, and the policeman thanked me warmly. He said that naturally the victims rarely reported such characters, and that they would be caught only by disguised detectives riding the trains in search of them and playing with notes whose numbers had been recorded.

Here in San Miguel the hunting of this kind is good. In the classes at the Instituto there are even in the winter a few sometimes talented young people with more courage than

money, but most of us, most of the time, are middle-aged or
older; some residents of the town but more transients, coming
from and then silently returning, after these little explorations
of Mexican life, and these little adventures into art, to God
knows what private lives in the States. At first glance most
of these people are obvious and depressing, but often enough
they will surprise you most agreeably.

Take the middle-aged and elderly women loaded with
beads, silver, and cameras, and flaunting girlish skirts and
exotic hats. Some of them shout rudely at Mexicans in English,
but many have worked hard and speak better Spanish than
you or I do. Some of them had husbands who earned all the
money on which they now live so well, and who dropped
dead on golf courses or ran off with their secretaries for
obvious reasons, but often these women have had honest,
effective, and even distinguished careers of their own. If at
the drop of a "Good morning" some of them will produce
photographs of their children and grandchildren, it should be
noted that they are not sucking the blood of these children
at home or pitying themselves. If, like mine, their water colors
assault the nerves and eliminate any but murmured and evasive
comment — what of that? They were perhaps more alive and
harmless while painting them than some of their counterparts
playing bridge or doing club work at home.

The men, too, with their peaked straw hats, their paunches
in the fancy shirts, the vacant, staring eyes, can be even more
depressing and baffling. Have these creatures been, until
recently, the operators of the United States, the strongest men
in the free world? A few, of course, are remittance men,
homosexuals, and what not, but more are nothing of the kind.
That tall character with the beautiful Doberman writes TV
shows, is probably one of the best dog trainers alive, and
during the war directed all the dog training for the United
States Army. This quietly dressed, reserved fellow with the
perpetual cigar, who struggles so doggedly with Spanish verbs,
was a combat general of Marines in the Pacific. That voluble,

red-faced little man who wears a bright green hat and loves to startle the Mexicans by raising and lowering the top of his new convertible suddenly in the main street shows fine feeling while playing Mozart on the piano, and his report on his recent exploration of Balkan and Russian industry is being studied by CIA. That handsome, tall, deaf old gentleman sunning himself on a bench in the *jardin* is still active as perhaps the best writer on science for the layman in the United States.

Perhaps our prize-winning specimen so far in this general field of the not obvious was a tall, handsome fellow of early middle age, dressed with negligent English male elegance, witty and seemingly cultivated, driving a white Fiat. This person let it be known quietly that he had earned enough in business (unspecified) to give all that up and study painting, which interested and moved him much more. None of us ever saw any of his paintings, but who can afford to be too suspicious of such reticence? If the business success seemed somehow doubtful, well, then, he might have inherited a fortune and been eased out of the Foreign Service, justly or not. The truth turned out to be even better that this: he was a penniless, perfectly healthy, and altogether first-class rogue in a great old tradition. He came from a textile mill family of the working class in a place called, implausibly, Moosup, Connecticut, or some such thing, and he had never inherited a nickle or done a day's work in his life. He had made a very good thing out of preying, tenderly, imaginatively, and ruthlessly, on women. Some of these, also in the tradition, who had discovered his true nature at considerable cost to themselves, still felt very tenderly towards him. In San Miguel and Mexico he got too many of his wives and other women too close together, and his necessary shuffling of legal papers became just a bit too complex and risky. He left suddenly, and the Fiat, at least, was seized by American officials at the border. Rumor has it that he will soon return, and although all this is well known here, I predict that he will cut an even wider swath. We men who try to earn a living and are unhappy when we don't are just too damned dull.

My bright hope now is an elderly gentleman, bald, with a fringe of white hair, steel-rimmed glasses, fine manners, and a New England accent, who often sits next to me in the painting class, and who responds to his own work with a gentle, self-depreciating chuckle. He may, of course, be only a retired and impeccable Unitarian clergyman, but he seems to me almost too good in the part, and his cellar in Pittsfield, Massachusetts, or wherever, could be full of female corpses buried nude in quicklime.

23. THE LITTLE MIRACLE

After the school collapsed here in San Miguel eight years ago, Leonard Brooks, in exchange for some literary help, gave me some lessons in organizing and painting landscapes in water colors. After we returned to the university, I sneaked, when I had time, into a few art classes, where I was helped especially by Dwight Mutchler, and I also continued painting in a desultory manner on my own. Returning to San Miguel, I have kept it up intermittently, between literary jobs, and during the last few months I have worked in a class in design under Jack Baldwin, who is one of the best teachers I have ever known. My pleasure in this hobby has been deep and increasing, but when I hear that there are now hundreds of thousands of us amateur, Sunday painters I sometimes wonder whether we know well enough what we are up to.

At first glance it would seem that this hobby is not essentially different from others, such as gardening, or cooking, or photography. Without injuring others, we amateur painters entertain ourselves, enlarge our sensual and intellectual capacities, heal our minds, improve our taste, and become more numerous and discriminating purchasers of the works of art created by the professionals. I still consider this view sound, but many professionals are objecting in private, and one, Brooks himself, has objected in public, in an amusing little satirical essay on amateur art that was published in the June 1955 *Atlantic Monthly*.

What these professionals are all saying, in one way and another, is that the fine arts are intrinsically so much more difficult and important than other hobbies and sports — even if you consider these arts also — that if amateurs don't take painting seriously enough they are not apt to learn or produce anything of value, and are apt to acquire actively bad taste. They say that anyone who thinks that in coloring areas by number, or in copying masterpieces according to some easy formula, he is making a picture is deluding himself grotesquely and lowering the general level of taste. If you cook a bad dinner, or shoot eighteen holes of golf in 120, you are less apt to deceive yourself and get false and destructive notions about the art of cooking or golf.

When I reminded Brooks that he himself plays the violin and the viola in public, if excellently, still certainly not professionally, he shouted, "Damn it, Allen, as a musician I'm more like Sir Winston Churchill as a painter than I am like your President as a painter: I *know* how bad *I* am!"

This answer, I think, reduces the objections to their valid essence. If he isn't going to insult the professionals and make a fool of himself, the amateur has to know how bad he is, and to know that, he has to study his art as seriously as the professionals do, even if he spends less time on it and has no economic interest in the results. Also, the more prominent an amateur is in other ways, the clearer is his obligation to do this, if only in the interests of the fine arts themselves. They are exalted manifestations of the human spirit, not to be treated like camp cooking.

This matter of taking painting seriously, even as an amateur, raises another point that is less often made, and that is that if the amateur approaches painting in this proper way he is

playing with fire. The more you learn, the more you see in it
still to be learned, and the more it absorbs of your interests
and energies. Also, unless you are very lucky, it may take
you a long time, while you allow it to interfere seriously with
your career and your family life, to discover whether you have
enough talent and enough serious artistic will to justify this
price. The other evening I ran into Dr. Olsina at the opening
of a show at the Instituto and I ventured to ask him for the
first time whether he had ever tried painting, in which I knew
he had a serious and informed interest. "No, Allen," he replied, speaking much more seriously than usual, "I think it
might well ruin me." Sometimes I have thought seriously of
selling this typewriter and spending my final days drawing
and painting, but I haven't done so yet.

For some temperaments at least, a certain amount of hard
thinking about the psychological processes of painting is
necessary to prolong and deepen the pleasure, and to keep the
road ahead open and free of blocks. Long before I began to
draw and paint I had looked at too many paintings of too
many kinds too carefully ever to be an honest primitive, and
if you have done that you have to keep thinking as well as
feeling your way through the aesthetic and technical jungles,
preferably with the help of teachers as experienced and as
honest as mine. I am now going to state my present, tentative
position as clearly and briefly as I can, for the benefit of
other amateur painters only.

The basic excitement of painting is that of imagining something new in the world that you just might possibly be able
to make out of something you have seen for that purpose only,
in terms of the medium you have in mind, and then trying
to make it.

First you have to enjoy looking at pictures as pictures.
Playing around with paint is such a pleasure in itself that if
you had never seen a painting in your life you might well
invent the art and produce something more interesting than
you are apt to see often in art classes beyond the kinder-

gartens, where the often more artistic results are uninhibited but accidental. However, unless you attached your product somehow to superstition or religion, or sold it, you would probably then drop it as a mental vagary comparable to doodling.

But you have to enjoy looking at paintings as a painter does, and that is, practically trying to paint them yourself, mentally, if you happen to want to, if the painting is related somehow, not obviously, to what you might be able to do yourself. This is the way I have read books for forty years, and the way I have now begun to look at pictures: looking for what might instruct and liberate my own different working mind. I cannot listen to music as musicians and composers do, and I cannot look at buildings as architects do, yet my pleasures in these arts are great. Therefore, except in art critics who cannot paint and in literary critics who cannot write creatively, I certainly do not scorn other approaches to paintings and books. However, I do think that the workman's approach to other men's work is the deepest and most satisfying. This approach is not merely technical, and so limiting. Only the fellow workman can see what has been done as well as how in part it was done. The danger here for the amateur is clearly that of imitating the results rather than trying to discover and re-experience what produced the results, and going on, in one's own mind, in one's own way, from there.

Next you have to play around endlessly with this medium and then that one, because the medium is not just a tool of expression: it is also, and perhaps primarily, an instrument of observation and experience. You have to see and respond to the object in terms of water colors, or casein, or oils, or duco, or whatever. Of course, painters make sketches in one medium and then pictures in another, but they do so like skilled translators rather than like the writers of Latin trots. The analogy to languages is fairly close, but in painting, the medium may affect the experience itself even more deeply than the language affects the experience of thinking, feeling, and writing. Merely because I have used drawing materials and water colors more than oil paints and other media, I am more apt to see a head, or arm, or hill, or flower in terms of a drawing or water color.

The "something new in the world" may appear faintly and crudely in your mind's eye before you go to work, and the result may even resemble somewhat that original vision, but most of the creation occurs in the actual process of drawing or painting. The moderns are quite right in insisting that the making of the picture — the organization of forms, lines, colors, and textures in relation to each other and to the dominant intention — is the essential process rather than the imitation of nature. For us amateurs especially, this organization is apt to appear only slowly, on the job, and I have been much helped by my teachers' urging me to try to make the

picture something interesting and good to look at from the beginning: a development rather than the execution of a concept. However, I still think that in good painting, even when totally non-objective, there is a kind of umbilical cord feeding the picture from the painter's emotional response, perhaps years before, to actual objects, and perhaps to very different objects from those painted. Otherwise the dominant intention becomes entirely too intellectual or merely decorative. The painting is not fed directly by nature, whatever that is, but by the painter's response to nature. It is, of course, very difficult for us — as it is for the professionals, too, for that matter — to find out which of our responses to nature, which of our dominant intentions in painting, are the most valuable. About my own I know almost nothing except that I'd like to paint and write like Mozart! And of course I don't know exactly what that means, either.

In other words, the painter's vision that provides the basic excitement of this "hobby" is not the practical man's or the nature lover's. It may be closer to the mystic's vision, but I am not sure of that. The difference is clear in painting the nude. It doesn't matter whether the model is an old hag, or even — if the painter is good enough as such — whether the model is a beauty and the artist loves her in the ordinary way and, like Renoir or Maillol or Lachaise, takes the dreadful risk of revealing some of that love in his work. What matters is whether he sees in her the possibility of an exciting but serene organization of forms, lines, colors, and textures expressing some visual emotion not necessarily aroused by the model and then has enough skill to make it more than a possibility, which might be almost as good hung upside down. I say "almost" because gravitation and the way our bodies work would alone keep us from turning galleries upside down.

It is a curious fact that in this very beautiful town and countryside, full of painters and students, almost none of the good ones are painting with much objectivity, with much representation. Of course there is some concealment of lack of skill in representation, and there is some faddism and some charlatanism, but mostly, I think, the good painters here are groping towards the expression of intimate visual emotions that may come from less obvious aspects of this fairy-tale setting, or that may come from experiences far away in time and space. I myself am happier when objects are sufficiently represented and identified to prevent groping and puzzling on my part, which can interfere at least as much with the aesthetic experience as literary content of a sentimental or sensual or otherwise obtrusive nature. Gradually, I suspect, the good painters here and elsewhere will regain confidence in their ability to dominate and use visually all kinds of objects that have other meanings and emotional effects than the strictly visual. For us amateurs a long bout of honest and good modernism seems to me a necessity, and I don't think I've had enough of it.

No amount of thinking and no amount of hard and happy work have kept most of my drawings and most of my paintings from being horrid daubs, and any amateur must expect this. The odd and good fact is that this seems to matter less and less as one goes on and very slowly improves. What does matter is keeping a sense of learning, of seeing new vistas open up. To this end I'm afraid that a few good and stiff lessons now and then, from a good painter and teacher, are almost essential. We can progress alone, and have to from time to time, but it is a slower and less happy process, full of pitfalls and blind alleys.

Jack Baldwin's classes, primarily in design or composition, have stimulated and helped me greatly. We cut out pieces of colored paper and paste them up in *collages* or shape and paste them into three-dimensional sculptures. We make things out of wire. We make drawings of such simple things as chairs, with a double purpose: to show a carpenter how to make the chairs and to show ourselves that this practical purpose almost requires a meaningful distortion of perspective. We have spent days and days drawing draperies, trying to simplify them and to use them emotionally. Jack sets up still lifes that are carefully disorganized, and then we work them up through many steps. Trying to remember and use all this under the greater pressure and distraction, we even have drawing and painting from the model. For me the two and a half hours of each session go like ten minutes. When they are over, I feel that I have stretched my mind most happily, and also as though I had run a mile. Studying under Robert Henri or Kaimon Nicolaides must have been like that.

In the past something like this has been done for me by sports, by the trickier parts of farming, and by navigation, which is a risky and absorbing sport that I will match with any other. Nowadays whenever I am disgusted by myself and by my writing I can always pick up a piece of paper and a crayon, or a brush dripping with some luscious color, and summon up everything I have learned, and then, even for me, often enough, a little miracle begins to happen. Usually I tear up the paper afterwards, but that has nothing to do with that incredible, almost musical experience.

24.   ANOTHER KIND OF HUNTING

For me, at least, this very subtle process of organizing a picture requires a certain amount of time, thought, and even comfort in some place where I cannot see and be seduced by the object itself, and where from six to a dozen people and burros are not looking over my shoulder. Therefore most of the very few decent drawings and water colors that I have made have been painted in my little study. However, these have been germinated and nourished mostly by sketches made on the spot, and now that we speak of sports, sketching outdoors is one of the best I have ever tried.

One reason why I have done so little painting in oils is that the gear is fairly elaborate to carry around, set up, and clean up afterwards, whereas drawing and water color gear is relatively simple. Except for a small folding stool and, when I need it, a larger board with paper stretched on it — instead of a sketchbook or a block of paper — I can carry everything I need very easily in an army knapsack that I bought for eighty-five cents. All the equipment that anyone needs is described and discussed in Leonard Brooks's book, *Watercolor: A Challenge.* Even when you buy the best materials you can find, as you should do, this hobby is much less expensive than photography or fishing.

My favorite sketchbook is an oddity that I try to conceal from the pros, because it looks so amateurish and pretentious, although that is only an accident. It is useful to have a sketchbook solidly bound in boards and leather and containing several kinds of paper, but the old man who used to bind books here in San Miguel seems to have disappeared. When Peggy and I were married, I saw somewhere in New York and bought for her a handsome, small (9 inches by 10 inches), blank book, bound in Italy in red leather, tooled. It was supposed to be a guest book for Oak Hill, but like most guest books, it was hardly used. When this painting mania seized me, I noticed that this book was made of paper that was very good for drawing and water colors, so I blandly appropriated it, and I have carried and used it in the queerest places ever since. When I glance through it, it shows me subjects and techniques to avoid as though they were dysentery and the pox; it shows that I have improved, if slowly and slightly; and it reminds me pleasantly of all kinds of people, places, and small adventures between the tropical coasts of Colima or Vera Cruz and Cape Cod.

The first sketch in the book, in charcoal, fixed, is of some mountains, and there are a number of others of the same object matter in different media. The problems here, as in drawing draperies, are to watch the hard and soft edges, to keep the whole thing bold and crisp, and somehow to use the material emotionally and pictorially. This point is made clear by the dullness of most photographs of mountains. The first picture that I ever painted that had some abstract organization was of snow and rocks in the mountains of Colorado, where the stuff abstracted and organized itself, but I imagine that the possibilities of such material are not unlimited. I gave this sketch to Alec Sturrock, of Glasgow, who was my good companion on a newspaper job, and I wonder how it would look to me now.

In painting the mountainous semi-deserts of this great central plateau of Mexico, it is better to work early or late in the day, when the glaring, dusty light of most of the day does not drain the colors and flatten out the forms. Frankly I have seen a good many paintings of this kind of country, vastly more skillful than mine, that seem to me, nevertheless, duller, suggestive even of picture post cards. Perhaps my lack of skill forces me to *state* something with the few words that I have. The colors seem to be chiefly the ochers of the earth and the blues of the sky, but there are many other colors in both, and one of the most true and exciting landscapes of this kind that I have seen was painted in nothing but reds and black.

The architecture of Mexico is suggestive and engrossing, but as always, you have to make something out of it, and that is far from easy. The things that I have done that displease me least are either careful pencil or felt-brush drawings, intended chiefly for learning and recording, or extremely rapid notations in wet water colors, with a few details drawn in India ink while the paper is still wet. I wish I could paint in Mexico with the bold gaiety of a Dufy, but if you think that style is easy and can be imitated by you or me, just try it. We went briefly down into Guatemala last year, and I was enchanted by the eighteenth-century earthquake ruins of great churches and monasteries in Antigua, which reminded me in that way only of Rome. The great broken walls and arches and mounds of earth and rubble, all working together, are very suggestive, and are easy to move around in your

mind's eye, but I imagine that endless quick sketches could become tiresome, and that real results would demand extremely prolonged and careful work at home, probably in duco.

I have a good many sketches of the tropical west coast of Mexico: clouds, mountains, and sea; beaches, lagoons, thatched huts, palm and banana trees; birds and boats. All of this is great fun, but as I glance at these sketches, it seems clear that for me, at least, the central problem is to avoid the obvious and the pretty. Once when we were down at Manzanillo together, Leonard looked at some of my work and then, by way of comment, merely painted a small picture of the harbor at sunset that was about two hundred proof corn. I hope eventually to penetrate the opulent, easy beauty of that scene to find something more interesting pictorially. Meanwhile I am endlessly fascinated by such minor challenges as the colors reflected by wet sand and the subtle and difficult shapes of boats and of birds in flight.

I like to try to draw the figures of people in motion — and if this be the inartistic prejudice of a writer, make the most of it. When Peggy is shopping she can always find a small

boy to carry her basket for a few *cincos,* and this leaves me
free to sit in the car and attempt a few quick sketches of the
people milling and sitting around. Working in the car can be
cramping, but has the great advantage of being invisible in
a country where many people are shy as well as curious and
friendly. Most of my figure sketches are crude or trite, but
every now and again I catch some gesture. Beaches are fun
because you can see most of the bodily structures of the
bathers, and the unconscious models fall into the most
amusing poses. Up on Cape Cod I seem to have been absorbed
by the gestures of the men digging for quohogs in the mud
flats, but I didn't really catch alive once that peculiar crouch
over the clam fork.

In every sketchbook you will find a few oddities that are
baffling or fun to look at later. Mine include: some careful
drawings, with dimensions noted, of pre-Columbian stone
sculptures in the public garden at San Andrés Tuxtla on the
east coast; a dowager with a pearl choker that I must have
conceived in a bad dream; a pet fawn at Manzanillo; some
little baroque sculptures in painted and gilded wood in the
museum at Antigua — how tremendously gay and sophisticated the originals were, although of archangels, intended for
worship; caricatures of my three women companions on that
trip drinking planter's punches and feeling no pain, and also
of Grace Kelly and the Prince of Monaco; and finally, a
careful study of a nude, who doesn't look at all like Peggy
or the Indian models at the Instituto, leaning against a bar
with a glass of cognac in her hand. Well!

Most of my sketching I do on my own, but several times
I have had the great advantage of going off with Leonard.
He is always working hard himself to store up material and
earn his living, so that he doesn't teach me and I am very
careful not to bother him. However, he doesn't mind my
watching him work, he talks about it afterwards, and although
he can go for hours and hours without thought of food or
sleep he is a very easy companion. One such trip that I shan't

soon forget was to a couple of almost deserted mining towns
high in the mountains on the border between the state of
Mexico and Michoacán. We were gone three days and two
nights, and into that brief time we crowded plenty.

Humanly these towns were depressing indeed: decayed,
more than half-abandoned relics of prosperous days fifty and
more years ago, before the veins of ore ran out and metal
prices went down. A few people were holding weakly on in
stores and cantinas, and hungry, sullen Indians drifted in to
trade a thin hog or chicken for what they could get. Visually,
with all kinds of weird forms and colors in decay, and with
a mountain backdrop, both northern and tropical, of unusual
richness of texture, these places were an exciting challenge.
In mood they were farcical and melancholy, pretty and
sinister.

The only hotel in the first town, where we stayed, was a
filthy dump, but we were the only guests, the owner and his
wife and thirteen children were most friendly, and the food
was decent enough. Years before, our room, which opened
on a balcony on the public garden, had been painted bright
red, yellow, and blue. For furniture it had two cots, two
chamber pots, and a peculiar wash stand. Of all this gaudy
squalor Van Gogh could have painted a fine picture, or alone
and insane, he could have killed himself in that room.

Before painting, we went to a pawnshop owned by some
cutthroats and spent a few dollars on earrings and woven
belts that those Indians make only for themselves and that
you could not buy on Madison Avenue or in Mexico City.
Then Leonard tackled a street scene with a house of a pecu-
liarly nasty green that he felt obliged to dominate while I
attempted a crazy, fascinating, wedge-shaped house of a
charcoal merchant, fit for some fairy tale. It was too picturesque for me, and besides, the background leaped forward and
smothered the whole, as though with an oriental rug. The
sky darkened, I rejoined Leonard, and we drove around in the
peculiar light, then tried to paint the rain coming up a street.

With this job, done frantically in five minutes, I was luckier than before. A couple of drinks in our sordid room, and I made a sketch of that washstand, which I loved.

Then dinner and out to a cantina in the dark, because the lights had gone off all over town. The town was full of grim little cantinas doing no business, but with jukeboxes blaring away (when they had current), perhaps to keep the town and the world from seeming too empty, too poor. This cantina was owned by a hawk-faced, middle-aged woman named Maria de Los Angeles. She wanted to talk, and we did so for hours, with her and with all kinds of very young or very old people who kept drifting into the candlelight from the street. Near the urinal there was lodged in the wall a narrow, horizontal shrine for the Virgin of Guadalupe, with one candle in a red glass, a crown of thorns, dirty pink and blue paper streamers, and dead flies. I lighted the candle, and Leonard made a careful sketch of this shrine on the back of an envelope. Finally we decided that the rain was not going to stop and climbed up the hill through a downpour to our beds.

The next morning we got off early, on a very rough road, to an older town, even higher in the mountains and more weird and sad than the first. This town was dominated by a good baroque church with a walled platform from which there were vast panoramas in all directions. Having learned to shun panoramas, I concentrated on a noble gateway and tried to remember how Piranesi or Sargent would have handled it, the latter in his luminous and authoritative water colors. I soon learned that these masters knew much more than I did, but I was not discouraged, and working like mad all day, I finally began to get a thing or two of which Leonard said only, "Not bad: keep going." Meanwhile he certainly kept going himself. One of his jobs that interested me most was of the market place in the strange light of a hailstorm. He worked savagely, while it lasted, under an arcade, with about a score of people watching him.

For lunch we found some good fried eggs, rolls, and cold

beer in a place in the market, and sketched even while eating. Afterwards we took a road up a hill, and Leonard nearly drove his car and ourselves into an open, perpendicular, abandoned mine shaft that must have been hundreds of feet deep. Half-naked babies and children were playing all around the edges of this horror. We pulled ourselves together and went back to work. When it began to grow dark, we started back to the first town. By this time I was exhausted, but Leonard stopped twice on the way back for quick sketches, and both times I went to work too. If he wanted to know when this amateur would quit he would find out. Even with our fatigue some of my best sketches, and his, came last. That night, in two more cantinas, we drank and talked most of the night with some friendly and curious men who operated a transformer station above the town. We talked about life, love, and international politics, and as usual, I found it much more fun and much more effective than any lesson in Spanish.

The next morning, however, our work began to go sour, so we visited the transformer station, as we had promised our friends we should do, and then started back to San Miguel. On the way home each of us made two more sketches in the mountains. By this time I had the trots, and also a queer feeling that I had to keep on painting to stay alive.

When we got home we found that Reva Brooks had brought the wife of a Mexican diplomat to drink tea with Peggy at our house. She was a fascinating woman who had served with her husband in Moscow and the UN, but very soon Leonard and I withdrew in favor of hot baths and early bed.

Some of the sketches that Leonard made on that trip, and paintings that came from them later, are now hanging in important private collections and in museums. These include the painting in casein that he made from the sketch of the shrine in that little cantina of Maria de Los Angeles. Sometimes I wonder how many of the fastidious people in the hushed galleries, stretching their souls a little before cocktails, have any notion where such beauty comes from, with what pleasure and adventure, and at what cost.

25. DEATH IS VERY CLOSE

Death is very close to us all, but Mexicans know it better than we do. It is for this reason, I suspect, that Good Friday means more to them than Christmas. Late in the afternoon of that somber day most of the people in the town, mostly in mourning, go quietly down to the open place in front of the church called the Oratorio de San Felipe Neri, hard by the market. Up from the crowds of people in the streets and in the atrium in front of the church rise the black cypresses toward the blue-gray, darkening sky. After a time a small orchestra and choir are heard from one of the courtyards of the church, playing and singing a requiem. Then there emerges, very slowly, a large and heavy bier, enclosed in glass and containing a bloody, bandaged, and shrouded effigy of the dead Christ. This bier is packed, inside and out, with small white flowers: gardenias, mock orange, etc. This is followed by large standing figures of the Santísima Virgen and San José, both in mourning. All of these are carried by the leading

citizens of the town, and the Santísima Virgen by ladies in
deep mourning with high heels that are difficult on the cobblestones. Among these figures are all the clergy, and behind
them come children dressed as angels and carrying on white
silken pillows the crown of thorns, the hammer, the nails,
and the dice. Behind these come the orchestra, the choir, the
two score of men and boys dressed likc Roman soldiers, and
the general public. During all this almost everyone in the
streets is on his knees. The procession goes a few yards down
the street — incidentally, defying the law — and then re-
enters the church by the main door. Then everyone rises and
goes either into the church to pray or quietly home.

I could be quite wrong, but it seems to me that Indian
dancing expresses a defiance of death. Again late in the afternoon, on the day when the great fiesta of San Miguel began
at four in the morning with a prolonged explosion of fireworks,
everyone goes down the road towards the railroad station to
watch the arrival of the Indian dancers. They come here
from Aguascalientes, and sometimes from Pátzcuaro and
other places, and they are met halfway on that road by our
own dancers, whose leader, an aging man of noble Indian
lineage, is the best metalworker in town. All of these hundreds
of men and boys, with a few women and girls, are dressed
in brightly colored costumes decorated with beads and mirrors.
On their heads they wear, above their own long hair or stringy
wigs, great headdresses of colored plumes and feathers. Beneath the feathers and beads most of the men are naked to the
waist and wear only shorts or loincloths, showing their lean,
bronze bodies. Around their ankles and wrists they wear
bracelets of shells — from which they are called *concheros* —
that add a peculiar swishing sound to the music. This is
provided by guitars made of armadillos, small drums, and
rattles made of gourds. I cannot describe the simple, powerful
tunes and rhythms that do not leave our heads and nerves
for days afterwards. The dances are weaving patterns of
motion — columns moving back and forth, in and out — with

steps that look easy but are not. They keep up this dancing in the *jardin* most of the time for two or three days, and the stamina required — possibly supported by marijuana — is incredible.

The two columns meet on the road, merge, dance, and then kneel in religious homage before an ancient stone cross carried by our dancers, and then all proceed up the hill to the *jardin* and the Parroquia. In the procession are carried great heavy frames covered with marigolds and other flowers, tortillas dyed purple, and golden chips made from the stems of palm leaves. These offerings, called *zuchiles,* are carried thrice around the *jardin* in the procession and then secured upright in front of the Parroquia. In the procession there are also usually included floats on trucks depicting an Indian prince enthroned in splendor, Conquistadors torturing their stoical Indian prisoners with fire and sword, and San Miguel conquering the Devil. All of this is done with extreme serious-ness, for the sake of the participants and not for tourists or money. After a while the curious gringos, not to mention the rich Mexican tourists who come for miles also, feel in their blood and nerves something that they also have inherited through centuries. After circling the *jardin,* many of the Indians go into the Parroquia, dancing, and fall on their knees. At the end of the fiesta, with their own cross and without help or hindrance from the clergy, they have their own final ceremony, dancing right in front of the altar. Now, as four centuries ago, "Thou hast conquered, O pale Galilean."

It is because religions, in Mexico at least, are so curiously mixed with each other, so vividly expressed in art, drama, and physical action, and so thoroughly soaked in the con-sciousness of imminent death that I do not consider it in-appropriate to turn now to another almost religious phe-nomenon of the late afternoon, the *corrida,* running of the bulls, *fiesta brava,* or — if you prefer — plain bullfight. I will not argue beyond saying that in my opinion, as a former breeder and feeder of cattle who has hauled plenty of animals to the slaughterhouse, the *corrida* is an art that can be objected to only by vegetarians, and that when it is good it is very, very good, and when it is bad it is horrid. Neither will I pose as an expert, because I have never seen a *corrida* in Spain, and in Mexico City and in the towns of this neighborhood I have not seen more than twenty-five. A couple of good if expurgated films and several good books have given many Americans some notion of this art and all the interesting things that surround it. I may mention that the actual *corridas* and several other scenes in *The Brave Bulls* were made here in San Miguel. Merely as an enthusiast I cannot resist mentioning a few great *toreros* and a few great moments I have seen, when death was invited and defied with style. I have to admit that if I have seen forty or fifty hours of bullfighting these moments cannot be added up to more than one hour, but for me they justify all the rest.

For education in this art the best *corrida* I have seen was a benefit performance given here in San Miguel for some honored and impoverished *torero* by four retired greats: our own

Pepe Ortiz, who lives here, Paco Gorraez, Silverio Perez, and
Carlos Arruza. Arruza had recently retired, fairly young,
with great fame, and bought one of the great bull ranches,
but the others, although in good physical condition, were far
from young; the bulls, although Ortiz's own, were mediocre;
and, most unfortunately, the great Arruza had drawn the
feeblest of the lot. Despite all this, for me, at the time, it was
like seeing a Davis Cup match after a few good collegiate
tennis matches. The difference is one of style, which is hard
to define in any art or sport, but that, I think, even the
uninformed can feel almost at once. Your great *torero* feels
out the bull telepathically, or at least with extreme empathy,
brings out the courage, dominates him, and all the while takes
the greatest chances with a certain silvery detachment and
elegance no matter what he may be feeling in his stomach
and knees. Poor bulls can be as dangerous as good ones, but
those four old boys of my age were as nonchalant, if alert,
as though on a round of golf, and their grace and precision
clearly hadn't come, for many years, from imitating others.
It was really a pity about Arruza's one bull that afternoon.
Whether he now wore a gray suit or not, his artistic pride was
clearly still involved. It so happened that afterwards Arruza
passed me in the narrow street, walking quite alone to his
sports car, and his lean, pale, and handsome face was still
working with disappointment and anger.

For the amount of time of distinguished action in one
corrida the best I have seen was at Irapuato, usually a good
town for the bulls, on November 20, 1955. It was otherwise
a happy trip, with good company from San Miguel. For once
the bulls were truly advertised as "six magnificent and beautiful bulls from the famous cattle ranch of Matancillas." They
may have scared the matadors themselves that morning in
the pens, because on their orders the first two were seriously
damaged by the picadors, but after the violent objections of
the crowd the other four were treated more carefully, and
showed plenty of fight until the end. Cayetano Ordoñes,

called, "El Niño de la Palma" — Mallorca? — was a con-
sistently good Spaniard, but not outstanding, and the rivalry
developed clearly between an extremely handsome and popular young Mexican, the son of another great *torero*, named
Juan Silveti, and a very brave, tough-looking, and skilled
operator named Guillermo Carvajal. It might have been
called the artist versus the more consistent craftsman, rising
this time into art, but the artist, Silveti, had more luck that
day. Time after time, with the casual elegance of a great
dancer, Silveti enveloped the great lethal black Beast with
Beauty, and finally, both times, with one thrust put his sword
into the heart. Then time after time the dogged Carvajal
equaled or surpassed Silveti only to have a bad kill. At the
end both were carried from the ring in triumph, and Carvajal
— who, perhaps because Silveti was so handsome and lucky,
had become "my boy" — was clearly astonished. We all left
the plaza with that feeling of catharsis and completion that
is given once in a while in the theater.

Luis Procuna is a big, handsome, temperamental man
who is justly known as one of the worst and the best matadors
in Mexico. Once here in San Miguel, at the big fiesta, we
saw both of these Procunas, and still another. The other two
matadors, Humberto Moro and Antonio Velazquez, were less
well known, but Velazquez, with both his first and second
bulls, was so good that it certainly looked as though he had
stolen the show from the great Procuna. With his first bull
Procuna was actually embarrassing because he seemed almost
as frightened and fumbling as you or I would be when faced
with two sharp horns propelled by a ton of bone and muscle
and savage anger. One fan told me that he thought that
Procuna usually underestimated the danger, with the result
that a sudden full appreciation of it would attack him with
double force. In any case, this time the crowd was less
charitable than this fan. This might be the great Procuna,
who had condescended to appear in little old San Miguel,
but San Miguel was having none of him. In the small ring the

critics called out their comments very clearly, and for throwing bottles two drunks were hustled from the ring, over objections, by the small but energetic policemen. After a bad kill Procuna left the ring in a daze.

Moro, and then the good Velazquez, and finally Procuna again, with his last bull, his last chance that day. The bull rushed in, and the moment Procuna, after watching his men test his hooking for a few minutes, stepped out in the sand, it was clear that we were going to see something very different. In the fading light the bull seemed enormous, not nervous at all, and intent on destroying his enemy, cape or man. Standing motionless wherever he chose to stand, letting the great, sharp horns miss his body by hairs, and weaving the heavy cape in the air in great, beautiful arabesques, the man dominated the beast completely and almost lovingly, talking to him gently and bringing out everything that he had in him in his last minutes of savage life. For a few passes we were all stunned, and then the *"Olé's"* broke out like gunfire. Every face in that ring was now alight with relief and joy. Procuna placed the *banderillas* himself, and each pair was like a couplet in a faultless poem. When the picadors came in, the bull tossed the first horse and rider into the air, and after the picador had been rescued, Procuna stopped it, as though as to say, "The neck is all right. Let us see the very best this brave bull can give."

When the time came to dedicate the bull, the matador did not dedicate it to some rich man who had supported him, or to the queen of the fiesta in her box, or to the whole crowd — all of which had been done before. He hunted down a rather ugly little girl who had been selling beer in the crowd, finally got her incredulous attention, and with grace and dignity dedicated what might be one of the great triumphs of his professional life — which might indeed be ended within the hour — to this unknown waif. The crowd, including me, adored it, but Procuna clearly didn't care about that.

Then in the last act of the drama something new came

out of the matador that must have been boiling inside him
since the first bull, waiting for the right moment. The first
few passes with the smaller *muleta* were even more dangerous
and beautiful than the others had been, but when the rhythmic
"Olé!" broke out again, an expression of insane laughter and
scorn appeared on Procuna's face, and while continuing to
dominate the bull as completely as before, he did not look at
the bull visibly at all, but grinning terribly, stared up into
one part and then another of the crowd, and once straight
into my own eyes, and began shouting what were obviously
the filthiest insults he could imagine. So we thought we were
critics, did we? Well, we could take a look at this. And so
we did, with a mounting agony of fear and delight, as the
arabesques elaborated themselves ever more beautifully and
terribly. Finally the bull was wound into a knot, and stopped,
panting, with a piece of the matador's coat hanging from
his horn.

Ignoring the din, Procuna turned his back on the bull,
stalked away to select another sword, and then returned to
his work. With only a suggestion or two from the *muleta,* he
got the bull's front feet together, sighted, and curved the
gleaming sword in between the bull's shoulders up to the
hilt. The great animal swayed a little and dropped dead.

Now every person in that place was on his feet shouting,
and the matador, standing there in the dusk, became the
center of a snowstorm of pillows, coats, hats, and flowers.
Once he bowed coldly, unsmiling, and then stalked to the
barrier while the crowd poured over the wall and the barrier
into the sand. Both ears and the tail were cut, but Procuna
held them in the air but once, to the *autoridad* only, bowed
with frigid courtesy, and fought his way out of the crowd.
I heard later that when men tried to carry him on their
shoulders down to the *jardin* he escaped from them into a
private patio and stayed there, saying no word but thanks to
his astonished hostess, until the crowd had gone. The old
fans were deploring the insults, but mentioning Manolete.

I am not quite sure what all this religion and art, this brutality, fear, and heroism, have to do with me, a little old gringo writer from Ohio. Do they have anything to do with you?

26. JAMES BOSWELL IN MEXICO

If you don't happen to like dogs very much, and think that many people are perfect fools about them, you can easily skip this chapter. Actually I think that people and dogs who are devoted to each other have a good deal more justifying to do than the other kinds of people and dogs. When there are so many children homeless and hungry, especially in Mexico, how can we spend so much time, energy, and money feeding a *dog* and trying to keep him healthy and happy? Is it chiefly vanity — the pleasure of having this handsome little creature love us and be dependent on us without making the demands that a child would make? As for Jamie and all other dogs, how can they desert their kind to the extent of giving greater faith and allegiance to these other animals who have the gall to act as their gods and who do very strange things to them? Well, we like it this way, we were made this way, we did not, for the most part, make ourselves or invent these strange arrangements, and we try not to be silly about each other. Besides, there is such a thing as being too damned logical.

Before Jamie we had many other dogs, and the last was a greathearted, intelligent, and absurd-looking cocker named Geoffrey, whom we sent to his death at the age of sixteen, when he had several incurable ailments and was mostly unhappy. If this was logical and even kind, that didn't make us feel any better about it. On his last morning he actually picked a fight with an old and immensely tolerant dog friend of his named Miles, and when we dug his grave in the garden at Oak Hill and put him into it we were both bawling like children. If you were completely reasonable you wouldn't have these beloved, short-lived friends at all; but then, for that matter, you wouldn't have any friends, or get married, or do anything else so foolish and interesting, except perhaps commit suicide.

A few months later, although we knew at the time that within a few months we'd be leaving home for parts unknown, we drove down to Cincinnati and bought another dog. This new pup was another male cocker, all black and four months old. We liked his looks and disposition, although he had a droll trick of expressing his affectionate excitement by rolling over on his back and urinating into the air and all over himself, in a graceful arc. He still spends a good deal of his time flat on his back, but early outgrew the fountain act. In fact, although only five, he now has a little white beard. His father, Champion Sohio's Gold Dust, of that color, was one of the handsomest dogs of any breed that we had ever seen. Peggy's mother and I had to talk Peggy into accepting what looked like a champion piddler, if nothing else.

We had him registered as James Boswell, and called him Jamie, because most of our earlier cockers had had names beginning with the *J* sound, and because we had been reading Boswell's Malahide papers with delight. We hoped that Jamie would not resemble his distinguished namesake too closely, and so it turned out. Our Jamie has done a good deal of traveling, he has met a good many "names," and he has had his erotic misfortunes, but that's about as far as the resemblance goes. He has a relaxed and healthy mind, and he doesn't intrude or — even when happily doing his tricks — try to "shine."

In his few months at Oak Hill he showed that, unlike all our earlier cockers, he was definitely a city dog. He had plenty of room to roam for birds, rabbits, and many other things of interest, and he had also an excellent guide and teacher in this older dog of friends, named Miles, but he soon made it clear that he would have nothing to do with

hunting, mud, or water in any form, and that he much preferred to sit on a dry stone and watch Peggy garden or go
to town and see friends. Miles taught him not to chase cars
and brought him up well in other ways, just as he had cared
for Geoffrey in his old age. Peggy and I are convinced that
dogs can communicate clear and fairly complex ideas to
each other without making a sound, and we think that
students of psychology, semantics, and extrasensory perception
could learn much from studying dogs and other animals.

After this short youth — and sometimes we feel he was
born a little old gentleman — Jamie took to the roads with
us in our station wagon, and he has traveled thousands of
miles since, on the whole happily. We make a platform for
him with his own blanket up in back of the front seat, and
there he can sleep, catch the breeze, take in the sights, and
bark at burros on the roads. He has his own traveling basket,
which he knows, containing food, water, rubber dish, comb,
brush, scissors, and eye and ear medicines. His injection and
other papers go with ours. Only in the late afternoon, when
he is tired, hungry, and hot, does he begin to grow restless.
Only once, in Memphis, when we were eating in a restaurant
that wouldn't take dogs, did we leave him too long in the car,
in great heat, and nearly knocked him out. He is always

delighted to get out of the car in the evening, get his food and water, take a short walk in the village square, and then duck under a bed and cool off. There can be scorpions and even tarantulas under Mexican beds, but so far he has been lucky.

There are plenty of cockers (more or less) in the big cities, and there have been a few even in San Miguel, but when we go into little villages down on the east or west coasts, or elsewhere, Jamie attracts so much attention that it can become a nuisance to him and sometimes to us. The moment we take him out of the car, in a *jardin* or market, a crowd forms, of children and then adults, at first silent and staring, and then asking questions.

"What a beautiful dog!" — "Thank you: we think so too."

"Is he very fierce? This is probably because of the leash, and for Jamie's protection we sometimes lie: "Yes."

"Is it a male or a female?" — the long hair.

"With permission, may I touch his ears?" — "Yes, but gently, please." — "*¡Fantastico! ¡Muy bonito! !Muchas gracias!*" — "*Por nada.*"

One man asked Peggy why she didn't cut Jamie's ears off, and she said, "This is not a dead bull, señor; this is my living friend," and that ended that.

And nearly every time there occurs this little dialogue:

"Please, señora: tell me what kind of a dog that is."

"He is a dog for hunting birds: a cocker spaniel."

"*¡Aha! ¡Es un cockair Español!*"

We used to try to clarify this a little and bring England into the picture, but since spaniels did come originally from Spain, we have given this up.

In the cities and in San Miguel there is a type of old lady, middle and upper class, who would never speak to us alone, but who can become very genial over Jamie, because these old ladies have had, or have wanted all their lives, cockers of their own. If we had working papers, and if Peggy wanted to operate a cocker kennel down here, I think she could make money. Nor should we feel badly about selling dogs to Mexicans who had enough money to feed them, because Mexicans are not as cruel to animals, we think, as they are commonly supposed to be. Food is scarcer, and children come first, naturally. Also, if you are going to defend yourself against ranch dogs, which are trained to be fierce, you have to throw stones at them.

Down on the east coast, as I've said, the sand was so hot on the beaches, for Jamie's feet, as well as for ours, that I had to carry him from the car. He refused to go into the water, of course, so we left him under a shelter for fishermen, and there, once, I found him sitting rigidly but bravely in the center of about twenty men and boys, who were staring at him as though he had escaped from a circus. That little black dog looked very far from Ohio.

Like us, he much prefers the west coast. At San Blas there are shore birds of many kinds in incredible numbers, and in chasing the willets and other waders in the surf, he never lost hope that he would catch one of those hysterical creatures. At Manzanillo his favorite sport is stalking the little ghost crabs into their holes in the sand. The last time we were there, millions of some kind of sea crab — which I have not yet identified and which was most disappointing when cooked — came inshore, apparently to lay their eggs. I found it fun to catch them in the surf with a kitchen strainer and then toss one up to Jamie on the beach. He would bark at it with hysterical pleasure for an hour and get his nose or an ear pinched only often enough to add to the excitement.

Last year we spent a couple of weeks with Peggy's family on Barnstable Harbor, Cape Cod, and there at last, there only, where there was no surf at all and the water and beach were cool, did Jamie discover that the sea was not made of acid. I got him interested in the horseshoe crabs, and then suddenly: "Look, Ma, I'm *swimming!*"

Jamie has one little trick, in the markets, that saves him from being too damned good. Once in the market in Valle de Bravo he walked solemnly up to a jug on the edge of a pile of pottery and, before I caught on, lifted a leg and filled half the jug without losing a drop. Everyone standing nearby laughed aloud with delight, but the sour-looking old woman who owned the pottery picked up the jug and smashed it on the cobblestones. We slapped Jamie, apologized, paid for the jug, and faded away. Once in front of the great cathedral in Morelia I missed, or he missed, by a hair, having to buy a whole big box of Chiclets.

Life in a Mexican house is rather difficult in one way for dogs, as well as their owners, because with open sky over the patio, which is tiled, and with flagstones running well out into the walled garden, how is even a well-trained and adult dog going to know for sure where he can relieve himself? Also, there is another problem, even when the dog has been totally discreet and found earth. Although many Mexicans and Americans make their servants chambermaid their dogs, that's *one* thing that the exchange rate will never seduce me into doing. In one of her women's magazines Peggy read about a gadget for this purpose, a kind of tongs, but that is just too decadent for me.

Jamie doesn't have too cabined a life in our house and garden, but the second big moment of his day comes soon after *the* big moment, his dinner, when it is time for him to get his walk in the streets. He knows the word *vamanos*, and is beginning to get a few others in Spanish, besides his score in English, and that word will send him prancing to stand at the door beneath his leash. Because he "stays" firmly, and minds generally, we can let him run free except among the cars around the *jardin*.

With strange people he is courteous but reserved, and he tends to avoid children, who often have been taught to throw stones at strange dogs. It always surprises me how many dogs on the streets Jamie seems to know personally. Not more than two or three in San Miguel have the hex on him, and when he sees one of these he walks carefully on the other side of the street, looking the other way. When one of these brutes jumps him, he gives an excellent account of himself until rescued, but then a few minutes later he is apt to sit down and howl aloud like a puppy. On most of the San Miguel dogs, however, including some huge mongrels, he seems to have attained a definite edge, and he takes great pleasure in stalking them and giving them dirty looks until they vanish and he can scornfully lift a leg, as though to say, "I may be 'that little black gringo with the ridiculous ears,' but take note of *this*."

For two dogs in town he has developed deep and totally unrequited affection. One was a big brown dog who took wonderful care of an old beggar in rags, with a white beard, who used to sleep in doorways. Nobody ever got near that old man, and Jamie, although quivering with hero worship, never got near his dog. Jamie still has a pathetic case on a woolly dog named Salaver — *sale a ver*, I suppose — "he goes out to see," but still gets the deep freeze.

I cannot take Jamie into my drawing class, because we move about a good deal and he would be in the way, but Peggy nearly always takes him to Dr. Olsina's class in intermediate Spanish, where everyone knows him and where his special friend, Graham Lewis, likes to confer with him on their common difficulties with *por* and *para* and the use of the subjunctives.

At six o'clock, after classes, we often take Jamie around to the "French Park." This is a shabby, romantic place with great old trees, fountains, beds of calla lilies, and thickets, all fed by springs. The other visitors are apt to be children playing or young men and women getting away together from their families and employers. Often the level evening light picks out the water of a fountain or some golden tree against the darks, and while I enjoy such things, Jamie banquets on odors and kicks leaves happily into the air. After that we often drop in on friends, and Jamie knows all their doors very well. He likes them and they like him, and he knows

168 AT HOME IN MEXICO

that when we have drinks he is apt to get snacks — legally, for doing his tricks, or otherwise, from some friendly *criada* in the kitchen. Theoretically we don't think much of dog tricks, but I must admit that Jamie enjoys his, as well as the rewards, and so do we. He sits up, jumps over our legs or through our hooped arms, and goes out of the room, "hides," and returns when called to find a cracker or other object that we have hidden in the room. Simple-minded? Of course.

No longer can I delay going briefly into James Boswell's love life, which is sad and makes us feel guilty.

For one month, when we were hunting for this house, we lived in an apartment house up on the hill, and at that time our friends Fred and Silvia Samuelson were living there also, with their little dachshund bitch, Tina Mas, of the Pintos' Mas family. Well, Tina was not only a charmer normally, she was in heat, and the Samuelsons felt no desire whatever for a litter of cocker-dachsies. That month was one long struggle by both parties, not only to keep Romeo and Juliet apart, but also to prevent Juliet's invisible signals from giving Romeo a nervous breakdown. The classical, frustrated lovers really had it relatively easy until their end. Finally we decided that we could allow the two to play together and did so, somewhat apprehensively. To Jamie, we could see, little Tina was as charming as ever, but where, oh where had fled the Gleam?

Soon after this disenchantment Jamie discovered that a horrid, fat, mongrel bitch, who lived in the cactuses down below and in back, was in one important respect, if in no other, just as attractive as Tina had been. How long did it take James Boswell of Oak Hill, A.K.C. No. S-518008, with sixteen champions among his thirty immediate ancestors, to say the hell with all that, and with romance besides, and to break for the stairs? The old bitch received him with warmth, but — he wasn't tall enough! Since the gardener who owned the bitch clearly didn't give a damn, I tried to assist, in vain. Soon after, she accepted the attentions of a Dalmatian. The results must have been odd in appearance, but meanwhile we had moved away, so I did not go out of my way to ascertain just what they were, and neither did Jamie.

Later a similar tragical farce occurred on the beach at Manzanillo, and this one was complicated and made more sinister for Jamie by the fact that the bitch in question, twice as big as himself, made it clear to all, day and night, that she preferred Jamie to the sixteen huge mongrels who were after her, while these characters resented the little black gringo to the point of entering our cottage and jumping him.

Once a physician here in San Miguel, Dr. Dobarganes, had several cockers and wanted to breed Jamie to one of them, but alas, they all died of distemper before anything could be done. A few weeks ago Dr. Dobarganes told me that in a neighboring village there was a priest he knew who had a cocker bitch and wanted her bred, and the priest had promised to let him know as soon as it was possible. We couldn't quite explain all this to Jamie, luckily, but Peggy and I went about for a while in an almost maternal and paternal glow of hope. When I met the doctor at a party I murmured to him, "Any news from the bitch?" "Ah!" he replied sadly. "The padre told me just the other day that some very common mongrel had just got her."

When the Pintos gave the Brookses their enchanting dachsie, Lucy Loosebones, she and Jamie quickly became pals, but she is just a child of frightening vitality who leads him around, literally, by the ear or crawls over his weary and recumbent form like a female wrestler or a diagram out of Van der Velde — or whatever his name is. When Maria refers to Lucy as *"La novia de Chemi,"* Jamie's fiancée, she has no notion of the irony. Incidentally, it is Chemi rather than Jamie or Jaime not only because of the phonetics, but also because she prefers to ignore the fact that Jamie has, most incorrectly, a Christian name.

He is, however, a Christian in character, and in one other odd way: I mean, since the blessing of the animals. This takes place in January, on the day of the animals' friend, San Antonio Abad, down at the little old church of San Juan de Dios, in one of the poorest sections of the town. It is at this church that Peggy and I find the fiestas more simple and sincere, and less aware of tourists — who indeed go there infrequently — than at the more impressive churches uptown. The ceremony took place on a balmy Sunday afternoon two years ago, and as usual, we had been advised of it by Juana in advance. With the Samuelsons and their Tina we took Jamie and went down to this church. Juana said that the animals would be dressed up, but the best that we could do for Jamie was a red ribbon on his collar.

In the little park in front of the church we found assembled a couple of hundred people, mostly children, with more than that number of animals on ropes and leashes, in cages, and carried in their owners' arms. There were two young bulls, several cows and steers, horses, burros, hogs, pigs, cocks, hens, chicks, parrots, parakeets, other birds, dogs, pups, cats, kittens, sheep, lambs, goats, kids, ducks, geese, and one white rat. We all stood around for a while getting acquainted with each other and with each other's animals. Nearly every animal had a ribbon, or a wreath of flowers, or gilded horns, or paper streamers. If they didn't enjoy the costumes and the gathering wildly, their people had a very good time indeed.

After a while a young priest came out of the church, and he looked sincere, tender, and reserved. His assistant carried out a table, and on this table were set up a crucifix and lighted candles. Facing this little altar, the priest read a few prayers, softly and rapidly, and then turned to face the people and the animals. He raised his hands and asked them all to come forward, and they did so, with a rush. Soon the priest and his assistant, a country boy, were hemmed in by a milling mass of people and beasts. The boy held a galvanized bucket full of holy water, and into this the young priest kept dipping what looked like a branch of lilacs, in half leaf, and shaking it over the animals while he kept praying to himself. He was careful, I noticed, to shake water on each animal that was pressed forward, and he had a smile for each child. While this was going on, two young bulls attacked each other, but their owners soon separated them.

Meanwhile I was having a little struggle with myself. I found that I wanted to get Jamie blessed, but I did not want to be sentimental, superstitious, moved by mass emotion or, above all, hypocritical. An American woman standing near me said to me, "More centavos from the poor! How cynical can they be?" I said, "I don't think so, madam. Look at that priest's face, and at the children's."

When everyone else had finished and the priest was about to go back into the church, I lifted Jamie from the ground and stepped forward. The priest noticed me and gave me a long, wondering look in the eye. Then, praying once more, he dipped his branch in the water and shook it tenderly over Jamie. When I thanked him, he responded with grave courtesy, looking me again in the eye, and turned away.

With Peggy's help I began to look for some kind of a box or plate, which had not been in evidence. When we found the plate, it contained a few coppers and a large white egg.

It has been debated whether James Boswell of Auchinlek ever became a Roman Catholic.

Twice we have taken Jamie on the long, hard drive back to Ohio, and every time he remembers several motels and a big mongrel who jumped him once at the Mexican customs in Reynosa. Visiting Oak Hill, he smells out all of his old haunts, and they clearly seem very good to him. Our superlatively good tenants there have an old dog named Spike, a Welsh terrier, civil enough, if a shade stuffy. Every time we are ready to leave after a call, Jamie cannot understand why we want or have to leave at all. He ignores us and the station wagon and lies down firmly on the old flagstones outside the kitchen door, where he and Miles were once so happy. This little gesture of Jamie's makes us almost more homesick than anything else. To this it should be added that when we return to San Miguel from the north he seems to know miles before we arrive exactly where we are going, and when the car rolls at last over the cobblestones, he leaps for the door with mad impatience and delight.

When Jamie lies on a ledge in the garden, watching Peggy at work and thinking his own long thoughts, I sometimes wonder how he and other dogs figure it all out. They have accepted us as their gods, and to paraphrase Dante, in our will is their peace, but we certainly do some strange things to them.

27. PILA SECA NO. 11

This is the address of Leonard and Reva Brooks, of their *criada*, Marciana, and of Lucy Loosebones. It is a very pleasant house, with an apartment, usually unused, down in front; two small patios crammed with flowers, vegetables, and an ancient grapevine; a central building with *sala-comedor* and kitchen downstairs, and upstairs, reached by an outer stairway and bridge, a handsome bedroom, bath, and *mirador;* and out back, a large, barrel-vaulted studio, with Reva's photographic dark room attached. We have spent many happy hours in that house, but they have just recently sold it, and will have to move out within a year, so that such hours in the future are now numbered.

I don't think the same can be said of our friendship with Leonard and Reva, but I am not at this moment concerned primarily with this friendship: I wish rather to fill in a little more solidly a sketch of a living artist who has already appeared fleetingly in these pages.

I first heard of this man in the autumn of 1948, when I received an unusually sensitive and intelligent fan letter about *R.F.D.,* which had been published ten years before, from this Canadian painter and former sailor who was teaching in the art school in San Miguel de Allende, Gto., Mexico, wherever that was. Leonard told me later that he never wrote fan letters, but felt a strange, not quite happy compulsion to write this one, and that he wrote it rather nervously, because the war had intervened and he felt that I might well have been killed in it.

In thanking him for his letter, I mentioned in passing that I had long been interested both in painting and in Mexico. I thought no more of it, but Leonard wrote again at once, suggesting that I get a leave of absence from my job and enroll as an art student in his school under the GI Bill, which would pay for tuition and materials and provide a decent living. At that time I was very restless in the academic life, and the idea attracted me greatly at once. Peggy was at first much less enthusiastic, but finally came round, like the good sport she is.

Part of what happened next, the bad part, is reported in the chapter in this book called "The Time of Troubles." The good parts were our deep pleasure in our work, in Mexico, and in our new friendships, the most critical of which, naturally, was with our sponsors, the Brookses. When, as a result of the political incident, the Brookses and the Smarts were broke and having house trouble — Pila Seca No. 11 came much later — and Colonel John Johnson and his wife offered us their house for several months, we promptly accepted their generous invitation. They were going orchid hunting and sea fishing, and the Colonel said that because of the recent

bombing of their sala by religious fanatics they would feel
more secure about their house if we should live in it, rent
free. The Johnsons' house, which was not bombed again, is
large, beautiful, and comfortable, and they had an excellent
cook and other servants. The Brookses and the Smarts were
in clover, and I must say that we made the most of the time,
in getting acquainted without serious rows, and in carrying
on all our different kinds of work.

After we returned to our job and home we kept in touch
with Leonard and Reva, and they later visited us at Oak
Hill twice. During these visits Leonard and I went out
sketching together in my favorite countryside; we gave a
private showing of his paintings to about two hundred of
our friends and neighbors, who astonished and delighted us
by buying many of them; Leonard lectured and had an
exhibition at Ohio University; and we were snowed in at
Oak Hill for a week. While Leonard was hanging his pictures
at the University he let fall from his pocket all the checks
that he had got for his paintings in Chillicothe. We found
them all, scattered down a stairway and in a wastebasket,
and I then kept them in my own pocket until I could get
him into a bank to cash them and buy traveler's checks. Like
other people who work hard, chiefly for fun, and who don't
worry too much about money, Leonard has the more devoted
friends and incidentally does fairly well economically.

Gradually, over the last eight years, I have picked up
some impressions of Leonard's past and notions about what
it might have done to his character. On the rare occasions
when he is in the right mood and company for reminiscences
he tells or invents stories about his past so well that I do not
propose to steal his thunder here. Perhaps it can be said in
general that, except for an honorable if pinched background,
he had almost no advantages, but early discovered in himself
a passion for painting, music, and books, and then tenaciously,
resourcefully, and on the whole cheerfully — with intermit-
tent fits of savage depression — made himself one of the most

valued painters in Canada and Mexico while still watching thoughtfully, from the outside, the art world of the United States. Like others of our generation, he found marriage and World War II major experiences, but has been very lucky. He and I share, among other things, an alarmed delight in Joyce Cary's trilogy about the painter Gulley Jimson and his friends, with whom, beneath our more respectable exteriors, we can too easily identify ourselves.

Leonard's body of work is of course the chief thing, but with my limited knowledge and taste I can only risk a few remarks on it. Several times he has found himself at a level of success on which he could have remained with some economic security, but only at the price of ceasing to grow as an artist. At one time he seems to have been a neo-Impressionist, specializing honestly in Canadian snow scenes. His work as a war artist, now in the National Gallery at Ottawa, I have not seen, but apparently he, like other war artists, learned and advanced a good deal professionally while risking his neck to draw and paint what he saw in action at sea. In moving from Canada to Mexico, he took a great leap forward in his work and produced a large body of Mexican landscapes, fiesta scenes, and so forth — including a series reproduced in color in a small portfolio called *The Posadas of San Miguel* — that, without his ever painting a political cartoon, made him one of the leading foreign painters in Mexico, respected by the great Mexican painters of different

schools, such as Siqueiros and Tamayo. This new work also
enhanced his reputation in Canada.

Finally, however, while he was being attracted and repelled
by non-objective painting, and disgusted and actually frightened by the chaos and the charlatanism of much of the art
world of today, his work began to slip into a romanticism that
seemed to me and to others skillful and charming but nevertheless a dangerous regression. Not being a professional
painter, I could not help him much except by listening to him
with real sympathy.

This listening of mine turned me into an early Christian
in a pit with two savage and hungry lions, one Leonard and
the other that very distinguished classical draughtsman who
has gone very modern, "superrealist" or "symbolist" or something, Rico Lebrun. Lebrun was attached to the Instituto at
the time. He was generally admitted to have more talent as
a painter, and more general intelligence, than almost anyone
in town, and he had a great effect — constructive or destructive, depending on the case or the point of view — on
almost every painter then here. Rico had respected Leonard's
talents, but had not had much effect on him, and they had
soon fallen out. Rico had liked a book or two of mine, and
wanted to know me, as I wanted to know him, but he quickly
decided that I was playing up to Leonard and doing him no
good.

Perhaps fortunately, I went to the States for several months,
and while I was gone I heard from Jack Baldwin that the
greatest sinner of them all, the final hold-out, Leonard, had
hit the glory trail and gone completely non-objective. When
I returned I found that the report was true, but Leonard was so
thoroughly enjoying his new period and I was so ill equipped
to criticize his new work that I refrained from quoting
to him his own remarks on non-objective painting of a few
months before. He and Rico were now the best of friends
again, and that was an excellent thing in itself. The Christian
now sat in Leonard's studio, happily ignored by the two lions

and watching them purr over each other, lick each other, exchange dogmatic and often brutal judgments on modern and earlier painters, and agree that no mere *writer* — even André Malraux — ever really understood painting at all. My opinion, which I kept pretty much to myself, was that Leonard's work at this time was very clever, basically cold, and in the long run dull; but that this period of his "conversion" would soon pass, leaving him a bolder, more solidly constructive painter than he had ever been before. So, in general, I think I can claim, it turned out.

A few months after Rico returned to California, Leonard suddenly hit a new low in depression about his work and his life, and pulled himself out of it only by painting a number of loving, fairly objective studies of the plant forms in his own garden and of various objects in his studio. Since then he has launched out in several directions, new and old, has painted some of the strongest and most subtle and moving of any of his paintings that I have seen, has sold almost all of his best work, and has written, on commission, his excellent new book on painting, for advanced amateurs, which I have already mentioned.

Deeper and stronger in Leonard even than his artistic ambition there is another, that in his early middle age has become almost an obsession with him, and that ambition is to remain fully alive until he is literally dead and buried. Vincent van Gogh was by no means the only good painter who has been consumed by a "lust for life," and no considerations of prudence, comfort, and even good manners put Leonard off for a moment. Growth in his profession, and in his reading and music, is not enough for him. When his home life or the company at a party seems dull to him; or when someone he is thrown with seems false and pretentious; or when some Mexican, Canadian, or American legal restriction seems stupid and unjust; or when some painter or critic seems petty or dishonest; Leonard is apt to go off in a boyish fit of the sulks or into a more respectable explosion of rage. Another

way — characteristic of painters and writers who have come
from solid middle-class homes and made similar homes of
their own — in which this lust for life finds expression in
Leonard is in his taste for strange characters, preferably
broken-down artists, writers, and musicians, for the dirtiest,
least respectable bars he can find, and for brothels visited
platonically for conversation with the girls and the madams.
He has some extremely rich friends and many extremely poor
ones, and he seems to prefer their forms of life and their
company to those of "nice people."

One evening I dropped in on Leonard with the unnecessary
excuse of consulting him about an automobile mechanic. For
a good many months both he and I had been working hard
and behaving with dangerously good if not quite exemplary
manners. After we had got rid of my car, he asked me to go
with him to the smallest, filthiest bar in town. There we got
involved, if pleasantly, in translating a letter that a ranch
hand had received from the U. S. Immigration and Naturaliza-
tion Service. For more privacy we moved on to a good, clean
little bar that is plastered with *corrida* posters, *banderillas,*
branding irons, ranch colors, and pictures of bulls and *toreros*.
There we got involved, if pleasantly, with the town's blind
singer and a couple of guitarists.

Finally we got off into a corner and released the birds that
were eating our livers. Mine was my resentment on learning
that day how an editor I knew and had previously respected
was preparing to dump one of his own authors who he thought
was "slipping." I did not know this author personally, but I
had admired his work for twenty-five years, and my identi-
fication of myself with him was clear enough. Leonard's
vulture was his familiar dread of death before death, and this
time it had an odd focal point and twist. I had showed him
that afternoon a clipping about the sudden death, in his early
fifties, of a college dean I had known and had once introduced
to Leonard. I had had no idea that this man had made the
slightest impression on Leonard — and perhaps he had not

actually — but I now heard a vivid lecture on just how this man's driving ambition, grim earnestness thinly veiled by jocosity, administrative talents — "always poisonous" — and even solid virtues had clearly conspired to kill him off so young.

We elaborated on these themes, and then moved on to related ones, such as just what kinds and degrees of neurotic bastardy and bitchery, if any, can be expected and tolerated in artists. My own theory is that although artists have their own severe occupational diseases so do dentists, corset salesmen, and all other kinds of workmen, and that any special standards of morals or manners for artists are inadmissible. Leonard amiably disagrees. By the time the bar closed — fortunately early in San Miguel — we both felt much better about ourselves, each other, and life in general.

On our way home we sat down for a while in the moonlight with our backs against a stone wall and our feet in a gutter. There we exchanged civil greetings with passers-by and speculated mildly on how we might get one more drink. Leonard usually has a much greater capacity than mine, so I was astonished when he observed placidly, "A very pleasant little debauch, Allen, if mild enough, considering the pale green chill of that moon," and then quietly rolled over and passed out cold.

28.   MERMAID IN JAIL

Many *criadas* are erratic, and many Americans expect too much of them, so that it is notable that the Brookses have had their Marciana for ten years. Every month or so her glandular and other ailments get the better of her, and she bursts into torrents of weeping, but everybody knows that she will be with the Brookses as long as they stay in Mexico or own a house here.

Marciana is a fat young woman of about thirty, with an open, friendly face and an endless capacity for little jokes and laughter. Our real affection for her and (I think) hers for us never leads her into the slightest shade of impertinence. Her major passions are for the Holy Family, her own large family, her señores, economy, potted plants, and the splashing of water. Nobody knows, of course, why she has not married. She must have saved a good deal of money and clothing, and be in a position to pick and choose. Perhaps she has seen too many wives beaten up and run to death with children, or it may have more to do with her glands and religion.

She is a magpie, and never throws away anything until Reva forces her to. Once when Leonard had torn up a lot of old water colors that didn't please him, Marciana secretly took the pieces from a wastebasket, pasted them together, and presented the results to a school. There they were hung until Leonard heard about them, removed them, and gave the school a good, new painting. Sometimes Marciana worries herself stiff with the notion that her señores are living beyond their means, and then they have to fight to get a good meal. Although she is not good with any animals except chickens, it horrifies her to destroy any living plant, including weeds, so that within a few weeks after the Brookses have gone to Canada you have to fight your way through their garden with a machete.

I have never seen Marciana more contented than when, barefoot, she is dumping water all over their house and patio and scrubbing everything down until water seems to be running out of the house's very ears. She really should have been born a fat little brown mermaid, spending her days scrubbing down the rocks just above the thundering surf, combing and braiding her hair, and singing to herself, with a tiny cross hung from her neck.

When the Brookses go away, Marciana comes to us with any problem that is too much for her, just as in our absences Maria goes to Reva. Until recently nothing really serious

has come up. To be sure, she won't spend a centavo of the money Leonard leaves with her, with strict instructions, unless we force her to; and sometimes we are alarmed when she removes the furniture from their rooms and paints, all over the brick floors, garish flower patterns in bright primary colors, but fortunately these works of art are worn away in a few weeks.

This last time, however, came real trouble. It began mildly enough, when Marciana was handed a notice from the tax office that said that unless the Brookses paid taxes and fines amounting to six hundred odd pesos within three days they would be evicted. I knew that they had been trying to pay these taxes for months, and that the fines were unjust, but after long conversations with the officials, in which I had to get an interpreter, I gave it all up and paid the money out for them as a loan that they repaid by the next mail. Meanwhile, however, Marciana was of course in a state, and one night about eight o'clock she came up to our house to be reassured.

That night she may or may not have negligently left the door of Pila Seca No. 11 unlocked. In any case, there entered the house at that time an intruder.

You will remember my mentioning a distinguished old

actress from Sweden. Well, this is Martha Hedman House, who used to be a woman of stunning ethereal beauty and who is still very easy to look at. When I was a schoolboy in Cleveland, before the first war, she was driving men mad all over Europe and America, and her reminiscences, pungent, humorous, dramatic, and never sentimental, are absorbing. She had rented the Brookses house for a few months, turned the studio into a handsome sala, had the garden cleaned up, and put Marciana on her toes. Because of heart trouble she went to bed very early every night in the lower apartment. At this time the household had not yet acquired Lucy Loosebones; if it had, the little dog would have earned her keep for twenty lifetimes.

On the night in question, while Marciana was up at our house talking to me, a slickly dressed young man entered Martha's bedroom, and when he found her there in bed, pretended to be drunk. Martha wrapped herself in a *sarape* and, with almost no Spanish or strength, but with great courage, somehow forced this man out of her room and then out the front door.

The next day she entertained Helen Wale, her friend Betty Ickes, and the Smarts at a marvelous luncheon outdoors under the grapevine, and in this Renoir scene Martha's story about the intruder, which she told with her usual gaiety and verve, provided a darker note. I honestly wanted to advise Martha to report the episode to the police, or to allow me to do so, and to be sure about the lock on the outer door, but Martha was talking rapidly, and advice from me seemed a little impertinent.

The next evening, Helen Wale had a cocktail party, and just at the time when Martha was telling a score of enthralled people about her sinister caller, he was back in Pila Seca No. 11 dumping all of Martha's jewelry into a blanket and then simply walking out the front door. Many of the pieces had great sentimental value for her, they were all worth about two thousand dollars, and they were very lightly insured. Marciana had left the house for not more than a half hour, on an errand, and swore that she had locked the door; and this was later substantiated.

The first we heard of it was the next noon, when a little sister of Marciana's, named Paula, appeared at our door weeping violently but unable to say anything except that she wanted me to go down to the Brookses' house at once. Peggy and I dashed for the car. The house was locked, with nobody at home, and all that we could find out from one of the small boys in the street was that Marciana was in jail.

We dashed to the police station, where I could find out almost nothing, and then I ran on to the women's jail. Meanwhile Peggy had found Martha somewhere and had also picked up Jack Baldwin. At the women's jail, a sordid little place down near the market, I found that Marciana was there, all right, being questioned by the police. I was not allowed to see her and talk with her, but I caught one glimpse of her, and she of me, and her face when she saw me made me swear I'd get her out of that place if I had to tear it down.

When Peggy, Martha, and Jack appeared, I learned the story. Martha already had a note from the Mayor's secretary requesting or ordering the Inspector to release Marciana. The Inspector was not on duty, but we found him at his house. When Jack and I gave him the note and explained that everybody had known Marciana for years, that we could all swear to her honesty, and that she had — believe it or not — never even had a boy friend of any kind to admit to any house, the Inspector replied coldly that if he released Marciana at the secretary's and our insistence he would wash his hands completely of the case and take no responsibility whatever for the recovery of the jewels. He urged us strongly to allow him to handle Marciana and the case in his own way.

This put Jack and me in a very tight corner. It was hard to estimate just how much Marciana would suffer by spending several days and nights, at least, in jail being questioned, but we guessed that it would be plenty. Another official

admitted to me later that the standard operating procedure
in burglaries was to detain the servants in the house until
they were "demoralized." Martha told us, and we told the
Inspector, that when living in another house in San Miguel
she had caught a manservant inspecting her jewels, but the
Inspector was not at all interested in that, or in my guarantee
to produce Marciana for questioning at the police station at
any hour of the day or night. No: our choice was between
allowing some very hard men to rough up Marciana and
losing, for Martha, all chance of recovering her jewels. This
seemed to us illegal, unjust, irresponsible, and lazy on the
part of the police, but there it was.

We finally told him to release Marciana, and Martha
quickly and gallantly backed us up. When we got Marciana
out of the jail, she was still crying in deep, sighing sobs, but
her chief interest was in getting back quickly to the house,
where she had left something in the oven.

The next day, Martha did not back us up or help herself
so well when the police sent her word to bring Marciana to
the station at noon for further questioning and she ignored it.
As the Mayor's secretary, who was having a row with the
Inspector, pointed out to me, that really cooked the case —
and, incidentally, quite discredited me with the police. However, as I pointed out to him, the police were ignoring several
possibilities, and had not even inspected the house or questioned Martha about the jewels and about the intruder. Also,
he or the police or both carefully ignored Martha's offer of
a large reward.

We consulted friends in Mexico City about getting a
private detective, but were properly advised against it. Martha
talked about taking some steps, through friends, to get action
from the state authorities in Guanajuato, but nothing came
of that. Jack and I had been almost too polite and tactful
with the Inspector and the Mayor's secretary, both, and so
when Martha read me a long lecture about the dangers of
becoming nationalistic in a foreign country, comparing our

conversation with the Inspector to an arrogant scene put on by Jed Harris or some other theatrical producer at the Orly Airport in Paris, I became almost as depressed as Marciana and as eager as she for the return of her señores. Still, Martha took it all very gallantly, and actually began to write a one-act play about it.

She moved down to the Instituto, and when Leonard and Reva returned, Reva quietly went to work. It appeared that when their house was being rebuilt one of the workmen — they felt sure without proof — had stolen money from Reva's purse, and this same man had later "found" their lost house key in a cantina that Leonard had never entered.

While Reva was finding out where this man now lived, the house was entered once more. This time, however, Lucy Loosebones, who weighs about five pounds but has a sharp bark, was on the job and awakened Marciana, who was sleeping in the house. The burglar escaped unseen, but this time only with a distinctive *sarape* and a *garrafón* of rum.

Reva had long interviews with the Inspector and other officials, and finally, at their request, she went with them when they went, armed, to surround this man's house. She says she was badly frightened, and I don't wonder, but she had to go to identify the man and any stolen objects found in his possession. He was asleep in the house under Reva's *sarape*. When he was "questioned" without any interference by anyone he confessed, reported an accomplice, and led the police to a place in the desert where they had buried most of Martha's jewels. Here they discovered that the accomplice had already dug them up and made off with them. He was captured also, but had already sold the jewelry, almost all of which was never recovered. In Querétaro they found a few of Martha's jade beads, which had been sold for a peso each. Marciana, of course, had never known either of these burglars, and the Inspector came as close to offering her an apology as he could or would.

It seems to me now that I heard at the time it happened

something about the "lost" and "found" house key, and that
if I had put my mind on the whole matter, as Reva did, I
might have led the way to the capture of the burglars in time
to prevent the almost total loss of the jewels. That kind of
intelligence and enterprise, however, is more characteristic
of the amateur detectives invented by writers than of writers
themselves. I deserved a lecture from Martha, but I got it
for the wrong reason. All I can say, and it means a good
deal to me, is that Marciana and I are very good friends.

29. LAUGHTER ON THE STAGE

In the American colony in San Miguel there is as much
social life as anyone normal could want or endure, and
perhaps a little more. Fortunately, however, almost nobody
cares whether he or she is invited to this party or that one
or not, and if you don't want to go to a party you can usually
say, without giving offense, that you are working too hard,
or simply that you have had too many parties lately. Every
once in a while Peggy and I give a large party, but our house
is relatively small, and besides, we much prefer small and
changing groups of from four to eight or ten people, in which
general conversation is possible, old friends can catch up, and
strangers can really be welcomed. Besides, in large groups I
am apt to find myself becoming neurotically frantic and drinking too much. What I really enjoy is when a few people drop
in on us in the late afternoon, or when Peggy and I take
Jamie and do the same to our friends.

These late afternoons and evenings in San Miguel, drenched
in visual beauty, and with nobody under great external
pressure of any kind, seem to me ideal for conversation, fun,
and friendship, and any crudities and failures here come
certainly from ourselves. Almost everyone has a garden,
patio, or *mirador* with plants and flowers, and with some

kind of a view of the ancient town in the evening light, or
merely of the changing sky, which is one of the many pervasive
and memorable beauties of Mexico. There is the old saying
about "dust on the heart," but for me it is clouds lifting the
heart. When the light finally goes, or the wind becomes chill,
we move into cheerful, comfortable rooms decorated with
flowers, Mexican antiques and oddities, and the paintings of
our hosts or of their friends and ours. When it is cold, there
are easy fires, and when the lights go out, as they often do,
there are always candles. When anyone grows tipsy, or merely
tired, he is always within ten minutes of his own bed —
provided he is not detained en route in jail. After the last
guests have gone, the host and hostess do not have to face
a mass of dirty dishes before going to their own bed.

Clive Bell has written that privileged ease like this is
necessary for the flowering of civilization. This I stubbornly
deny because I have known some very hard-pressed yet very
civilized people, and because any civilization based on privi-
ledge cannot seem to me, a radical democrat, wholly fragrant
and a final good. I will admit that, considering our advantages,
our social life could reasonably be judged by very high
standards. I am not myself sufficiently civilized to make such
a judgment. All I can say is that here in San Miguel I have

heard some first-class talk by unusual and engrossing people, and have seen some very adult and graceful behavior under pressure. We have our bores and our boors and our neurotic messes, but they do not often set the tone.

My impression is that our little society is more interesting than that of an average American country club set, and more closely comparable to that of a good college faculty. When I say this I hasten to add that we are naturally somewhat overweighted in the arts and in Spanish; that rank, seniority, and tenure do not exist; that there is no administrative leadership or pressure; that ambitions do not exist in relation to the group; and that we are stimulated by an unusual number of transients of interest and distinction. Our society is more highly flavored because, quite aside from the exchange rate, everyone living here is for the time being, at least, a misfit in the United States, but has taken steps to find and make his own life. Despite the respectable appearance of some noon coffee parties, for example, we lack the timidity of many professors and other employees, and are certainly not a group of sweet old ladies and gentlemen in Cranford. This courage is not based entirely on some economic security: plenty of people are living here, with risk, on what would be frayed shoestrings anywhere.

This whole estimate may be a little generous, but I don't think it is.

In this social milieu, as in others very different, such as that of farmers and their families in southern Ohio, Peggy and I have been lucky enough to find some friends whom we wear in our hearts' cores, and whom we'd like to keep all our lives. A number of these have already appeared, fleetingly or at greater length, in these pages — but not necessarily in accordance with their personal importance to us; and there are others equally dear not even mentioned. It must not be inferred from Chapter 22 that I merely collect people as specimens. In friendship as in love mutual study and amusement are necessary, but mutual need is the core. Like you

and everyone else, I need people something but not too much like myself to share their good and bad experiences and mine; to broaden, deepen, and refine life; and to feel somewhat less alone and pointless this side of the grave. I can well understand why all kinds of people, everywhere we go, enjoy and need Peggy, but I am sincerely surprised and pleased when I discover, from time to time, that someone actually needs and enjoys me. I am not very helpful or ornamental, wise or witty; I have all kinds of unpleasant habits; and much of the time, in my own unimportant way, I am off in a daze of contemplation.

Although friendship is very important to me in the normal way — if less so, I claim, than to those who are always expectant and sucking — it is also important to me in another way perhaps a little less common: I enjoy friendship increasingly as an adventure, with all its odd twists and vagaries.

To discover suddenly that this person, of whom one would certainly not have expected anything of the kind, has a fresh idea about the drawings of Géricault or Steinberg, or was a hundred yards away, in command, on that bad night on that beach in New Guinea; to say good-by to a friend before a long separation, wondering, and to meet again, after years, and then find that it is as good as ever, or better, or else that all really ended long ago and meant only so much; to discover that this weak and dull old acquaintance actually lives in one unsuspected area with courage, freshness, and style, or that this other friend, who seemed so strong and wise, is

eaten hollow inside by vanity, or by some deeper hunger and
frustration, and is in dreadful pain; to discover without any
possible doubt that some pal of years, coming to dinner that
night, just the other day calmly forged a signature or lifted
an article from a counter; suddenly, without cause except in
one's own mysterious and treacherous mind and heart, and
quite without excuse, to resent bitterly some innocent old
friend, or to imagine quite vividly some other old friend in
bed — all such experiences are commoner than they are
supposed to be, and for me they form no small part of the
comedy, the terror, and the wonder of life, here in San Miguel
or anywhere else. If this be romanticism, make the most of
it. Clear good sense, that invaluable instrument, can turn
everything into comedy, and sometimes even into noble music,
but it has to be broad, alert, ready for anything, and is far
from equivalent to practicality, or prudence.

When we are at our best, something sometimes happens
on this peculiar stage that I find profoundly exhilarating, and
that is when two or even three of us, almost at the same
time, suddenly see through each other a little further, stare
a moment perhaps in pain, and then break out in honest,
loving laughter.

30. OUR LADY OF SOLITUDE

Every night during the week before Christmas a parade goes
down one of the streets of San Miguel that has been announced
in advance and decorated for the occasion by its householders with stalks of bamboo and paper lanterns and
streamers. This procession consists of the town band; floats
on trucks depicting the Nativity; trucks full of children
dressed conventionally as *pastores*, or shepherds, and singing
their heads off; men and boys carrying lighted lanterns shaped
as large red and gold stars; others carrying large, clownish,

surrealistic heads made of papier-mâché; and the general
public trooping along behind or getting mixed up with everything else. The floats of the Nativity are constructed with
loving care, complete with living sheep and goats especially
cleaned for the occasion, and the young people taking the
parts of the Virgin, San José, and attendant angels bear
themselves with unfailing dignity. As the procession slowly
moves on, colored fires and rockets break out from the
nearby roofs, and the narrow street now glows like a core
of fire in the surrounding darkness.

These are the famous *posadas,* which means inns, because
up until recently the whole procession was a dramatic
depiction of the fruitless search of Our Lady and San José
for a room at an inn in Bethlehem; but, except in our little
street, this essential part of it now seems to have been lost in
the excitement. It is the custom for householders to have
prepared and hanging above the street *piñatas* full of candies
and fruits for young children, but during the last few years
crowds of young hoodlums have broken these in advance, so
that now policemen have to be on hand to guard the procession. In short, as everyone observes sadly and probably
truly, the *posadas* of San Miguel will never again be as
reverent and beautiful as they used to be.

Therefore Peggy and I were happy to discover that in our
little street, the Callejón de Calvario, much of the old spirit
had been kept alive. Led by Don Carlos and by Eufemio
Rodriguez, an attractive and talented young man of the
street, our neighbors decorated it very gaily, and I did what
I could to help. Then every evening at dusk, long before
the *posadas* were moving elsewhere, we had our own. Our
little procession consisted of the children of the street, with
others from the neighborhood, forty or fifty in all, each
carrying a lighted candle, and all singing under the leadership
of Señor Rodriguez, a charming old man on crutches, and of
a young man, Señor Cruz, who sings regularly in the churches.
At the head of the procession there was carried a small

scene of the Flight into Egypt, and everyone told us proudly that the really beautiful little figures, wearing little straw hat like *campesinos,* were extremely old. When the procession reached the steps and doors of the ancient little chapel of Our Lady of Solitude, on the corner, the doors, now used as those of an inn, were closed. An appeal for a room was sung, and then someone replied, also singing, from inside that there was no room. After several exchanges the doors were opened, the little figures were placed before that of Our Lady, and everyone knelt to pray and sing. This figure is four hundred years old, carved of stone, and dressed in black and silver. She looks very much like Queen Victoria in old age.

Every evening after this service the Holy Family was returned carefully to the house in which it was kept, and then all the children repaired to the front of Don Carlos' shop to break a *piñata* or two provided for that night by one of the neighbors. This is always done by blindfolding one child after another, giving him a stick, turning him around several times, and then letting him go to work. As he strikes madly this way and that, the men holding the *piñata* suspended by ropes keep raising and lowering it, and everyone shrieks with laughter. Finally some child is allowed to break the *piñata,* and then the children all scramble for the candies and fruits. These mean more to these children than they would to children in the States, but always the older ones take very good care that their little brothers and sisters get their share.

On their way home many of them stop once more to look again at the Nacimiento that we have set up in our front window. We did this rather late, but were lucky to find all the little figures that we needed and a charming little thatched stable above the roof of which Our Lady had hung out her wash at the last minute. Peggy surrounded this with moss and little plants, and above it she hung on threads little white doves that fluttered in the warm air rising from the candles. Maria was delighted with all this, and insisted that the Niño Dios be properly swaddled and that He should not put in His appearance until the moment after midnight on Christmas morning. Closest to Our Lady, among the other animals, we put a little china figure of a black cocker spaniel that Peggy's

mother had given her, and we were delighted when all the
children kept pointing out to each other, "Look! There's
Chemi, too!"

Soon after Christmas the entire, large Rodriguez family
went to work on a *colóquia* that they planned to put on, on
the day of the Three Kings, January 6, right in our street.
The only way in which I could help was in loaning some
lumber for the stage. As I have said, the *colóquias* are a close
Latin equivalent of the English mystery plays that were put on
five and more centuries ago, with all kinds of low comedy
and pretty dancing introduced into the Christmas story, and
Señor Rodriguez was able to write out all the parts for this
three-hour production from memory. This was the funniest,
prettiest, and least tedious *colóquia* Peggy and I had seen —
but of course we could have been prejudiced. The Rodriguez
family and other neighbors were the producers, and took
many parts, but they also had the help of friends from the
ranches who had experience and talent, if no more zest. What
we enjoyed most were the "morris dances" and some of the
jokes. For example, when the figure who, dressed in a vivid
red robe and a crown, combining Herod and Satan, was
informed that the Christ was about to be born, his fear and
rage were awful to behold, and he cried, "But this is terrible!
Where is my lawyer?"

That is the evening, not Christmas, when gifts are given
to children, and we had ready a couple of large baskets of
fruit, candy, and sugar cane, which Maria parceled out at
the door. After it was all over, I also gave the theatrical
company a *garrafón* of rum.

Peggy and I are very happy to know our neighbors as well
as we can, and to be accepted by them, and we wouldn't live
anywhere else in town, but there is a cloud over our little
street, our chapel, and Don Carlos' shop. The chapel and
shop are located right at the corner of the main street of the
town, where it swings at right angles up a steep hill and
becomes the road to Querétaro. Trucks, buses, and other

cars coming down into town have to take this corner very carefully, and most of them know it, but as in the States, all brakes are not good and all drivers are not always sober.

We had heard of previous accidents, and once when we returned from a trip somewhere we found all of our neighbors depressed by a more recent horror. One night a truck out of control had smashed into the portico of the chapel and killed almost one whole family, with its burros.

Then one evening recently, driving up the main street, we were stopped by police and a crowd, and we could see that another accident had taken place on nearly the same spot. Terrified for the Quintanars, other neighbors, and the shop, we left the car and rushed up the hill. No friends of ours had been touched, which was a great relief, but it was brutal just the same.

Another truck out of control, full of sacks of beans and country people, had smashed into the front of the Quintanars' house. One man had been killed outright, and several other people, including children, had been seriously wounded. By the time we arrived, the dead and wounded had been removed, and we heard later that Drs. Alsina and Dobarganes had worked on the latter in the wretched little town hospital most of the night. Everyone said that the police had found the brakes of the car in order, and that immediately after the accident the driver, evidently drunk, had leaped from the car and escaped up our street in the direction of open country.

In the Quintanars' shop, in their care, there sat a weeping little girl of eight or so, the daughter of the man who had been killed. Peggy gave Don Carlos' mother money to help with her care and transportation back to her home in a neighboring town, and a few days later, to our surprise, we received a formal letter of thanks from the City Hall. One man riding on top of the load was catapulted right through the wood and glass of Don Carlos' unbarred windows into the center of his large sala, but was almost unharmed.

The chapel steps and Don Carlos' store, which has doors

large enough to admit a truck, are often crowded with people, and these dreadful accidents could keep on happening indefinitely. That night I urged him to build a steel and concrete barrier in front of his shop. He said that he had thought of doing so, but with the entrance to our street, which we call "the slot," being hardly wide enough for a car, such a barrier would bar the street to all traffic, including my car, the only one owned on the street. I protested that this was relatively unimportant, but he said that, in any case, he doubted that the city authorities would give him permission. He has since talked of moving the shop to another room in the house and building a barrier inside the present entrance, but he has no more loose money than anyone else. The officials have talked about rebuilding a colonial road into the town from another direction and forcing all trucks and buses to take that, but it could take fifty years for anything like this to be accomplished.

Meanwhile I think sometimes about that tender, sorrowing, fat, very old Lady of Solitude, who receives the sincere and graceful worship of all these people and their children within a few feet of this bloody spot. I wish that I felt — as probably Maria does — that if we were good enough she could do something about it.

31. AN EVENING AT MANZANILLO

One afternoon nearly three years ago when we were swimming on the great beach at San Blas, a small American schooner appeared and anchored in the difficult channel. She was a yacht with auxiliary power, and a beauty. There were very few foreigners in the village, so we were not surprised when in a little restaurant we met the owner and skipper, his wife, and their friend, another middle-aged man. All three seemed competent and alert. A paid hand, just out

of college, had been left on board. The skipper, Dr. Holcomb, was a retired physician from Oakland, California, and their friend was a physician from New York. All three had had a good deal of experience of both racing and cruising. They were bound for Manzanillo, Acapulco, Panama, Peru, the Galápagos Islands, Pitcairn Island, Tahiti, and so on, around the world. They expected to spend at least two years on the voyage, but the New York doctor had to return from India by liner. We were going to drive soon down to Manzanillo, and we were happy when they asked us to come aboard if we should meet there.

We met the Brookses at Manzanillo and shared a cottage on the beach for several wonderful weeks of painting and loafing. The *Landfall* did not appear in the harbor, and we assumed that she had skipped Manzanillo and gone straight on to Acapulco. However, one afternoon Peggy and I went up the coast to the beach at Santiago and, to our delight, found the *Landfall* anchored there and her crew just finishing dinner at the hotel on the beach. They greeted us warmly and took us and Jamie aboard in their small plastic boat.

Jamie acted as though we were about to throw him to the
sharks, but cheered up when he got aboard and found on the
deck a big sea turtle lashed there on his back. Other guests
were a rich Mexican rancher from near Celaya, his pretty
wife, and a very correct couple from New Jersey. We all had
a swim, followed by drinks in the cockpit. The skipper produced a ukulele, of all things, and sang many songs that
were witty and often bawdy. It was a very odd collection of
people, but we all got along surprisingly well.

When the skipper took us around, it was clear that the
Landfall was the finest cruising yacht we had ever seen. There
wasn't a piece of brightwork or unnecessary gadgetry in sight,
everything was functional and of the highest quality, and
there were more room and comfort than anyone could
decently expect. She had a good diesel engine, storage bat-
teries that looked fit for a submarine, and good radios, including a transmitter. The navigational gear was almost as good
as what we had in the LST's. The galley, john, bunks, and
so on, had, like everything else, been given great thought
to produce the best results with the fewest complications. I
had some doubts about the nylon lines, but kept them to
myself, because that skipper clearly knew much more about
everything than I did. Repairs, fuel, water, storage, fishing
gear: I couldn't think of a thing that this sailor hadn't solved
perfectly, as far as I could tell. He told me that he had
bought the schooner from a movie star and then spent a year
of hard work — and, I thought to myself, a small fortune —
fitting her for this voyage. They had, of course, a complete
and up-to-date collection of almanacs, sailing directions,
astronomical tables, and so forth — he used H.O. 211, as
I remember it — but for our part, we should have enjoyed
a few more reading books. When we asked, the skipper's
wife said yes, they'd be delighted to take any books and
magazines we cared to get rid of, so when we went ashore
we sent back a collection.

That evening, we went with the Brookses to a place on the

inner, lagoon side of Manzanillo where the lagoon is connected with the sea by a channel that runs through a large
tunnel through one of the hills of the town. When the tide
is coming in, that place is always crowded with men, women,
and children all fishing from skiffs, from the beach, and from
a rickety wooden bridge. Some use lines, some cast large
circular nets very adroitly, and some frogboys with goggles
leap into the channel with spears and come out almost every
time with impaled and struggling silver fish. That night,
there was a huge, pale orange, full moon; rising steeply from
the water, the whole town was alive with paper lanterns like
glowworms; and along the margins of the channel and the
lagoon there flickered, reflected in the water and shining on
the dark, wet bodies of the fishermen, scores of little kerosene
flares that they were using to catch shrimps with their hands.
At one end of the bridge there rose the dark forms of thatched
huts with palm trees. Over it all there was a murmur of soft,
excited voices, and the soft sea air was rich with odors.
Leonard made some rapid pencil notes, and the next day
painted a handsome picture from this scene, subdued and
suggestive, in the oriental manner, but that time I couldn't
do anything but stand there in a daze.

When we went back to the beach, Leonard and Reva went
to bed, but Peggy and I had a swim, naked, in the moonlight.
Without ever being cold, the water there is always cooler than
one remembers, very invigorating, and that night it was

full of phosphorescence that made our whole bodies glow pale green. When we came out of the water we sat for a while in our bathrobes on the porch of the cottage listening to the long sighing of the surf and looking out across the dark, moonlit water towards Tahiti.

We talked about the *Landfall* and her crew, our friend Bill Crosby's ketch, the *Sea Dawn,* the cruise we had had in her, with Bill and Helen the summer before, down the coast of Maine, the dreams we elaborated that summer of cruising together down through the Windward and Leeward Islands, my days and nights in the Southwest Pacific, Captain Bligh and Fletcher Christian, Paul Gaugin reaching his peak and rotting with syphilis, and the young Joseph Conrad with his first command.

That afternoon, the college boy in the *Landfall* had been eager to get into the mail a letter to his girl in California, and we wondered how long he would keep writing to her and she to him. We also wondered why the skipper had left his practice, where all the money came from, and just what kind of people these were to hunger not only for landfalls and exotic harbors, but also for departures and for endless, fighting days and nights in heavy seas and under sunless and starless skies. That schooner was perfect of her kind, and those people were sailors and no fools, but there would always be the possibility of their suddenly gurgling out their lives, and of their bodies then sinking down and down into the dark. Perhaps they preferred that to the equally good chance, in Oakland, of having the world disappear suddenly in a taxi or on a golf green and then being turned over to the malodorous ministrations of the undertakers' boys.

Then how did they enjoy their romantic, boyish play — for it was that, however demanding — while millions of children had to sweat, starve, and rot with disease that they could cure, with very little play at all? And for that matter, how did we enjoy our own play with flowers and paints and words — while twenty-odd children in our own street had so little food, medical care, and education? Well, how did we know that one of those people wouldn't write a tale of that cruise that would enchant a million boys and girls who could never leave their home towns? Besides, we had been advised to consider the lilies of the field. That was, of course, the last excuse of the parasite, but if men and women were good enough, in one way or another, there might be something in it, and to take that little schooner around the world these people were very good indeed. As for ourselves, I reminded Peggy that she had her Biblioteca, and I told her that if people didn't want to buy the only wares I could produce — little essays about this and that — the more fools they. I reminded her that the author of *Gulliver*, still enjoyed by children and others, had not lived on his royalties from that book, and meanwhile had been a damned neurotic, parasitic, and reactionary politician, and a political clergyman besides. Peggy laughed and shut my mouth, at last, with hers.

The next morning, I wakened early, and when I stepped outside I could just see the tiny white sail of the *Landfall* disappearing in the pearly, misty, morning light. Months later, from Tahiti, we received a kind post card, and long after that another one, from a little harbor in England.

32.   THE SENSE OF THE PAST

The Church is much more powerful and omnipresent here on the high plateau of central Mexico that it is down on the east and west coasts and elsewhere, and it is especially powerful in San Miguel; yet since 1810 all of these towns have been involved in the War of Independence, the Reform, and the Revolution, and this town is not apt to forget that its full and proud name is San Miguel de Allende.

In 1810, Ferdinand VII of Spain and his family were in prison, Joseph Bonaparte ruled ineptly in Madrid, a *junta* in León represented independent Spain, and all of Latin America was coming to a boil of revolt. In most Latin-American countries the creoles, or native-born whites, were the leaders of rebellion and remained in control. In Mexico, accidentally and prematurely, the deeper forces of the Indians and the *mestizos,* or half-breeds, were released, so that here the creoles allied themselves with the *gachupínes,* or Spaniards, the struggle for independence became a bloody class war, and it was for decades ineffective.

This accident occurred in Querétaro, San Miguel, and Dolores. The leading conspirators for independence were intellectuals, aristocrats, a few army officers, and a priest sympathetic with the Indians. In Querétaro the leaders were the Corregidor, or Chief Magistrate, and his wife, and when the conspiracy was discovered, the latter managed to send a messenger, with the news and warning, to their ally here in San Miguel, a young army officer, aristocrat, and fan of the bulls named Ignacio Allende. The messenger arrived at about eleven o'clock on the night of September 15, and Allende rode at once to Dolores to warn another leading conspirator, Father Miguel Hidalgo y Costilla. Hidalgo managed to arrest all of the *gachupínes* in Dolores, and the next morning rang his church bell and to the assembled populace cried out the Grito de Dolores, proclaiming the independence of Mexico. It was now too late for Hidalgo and Allende to win over more creoles and army officers. They could appeal now only to landless Indians, and a mild revolution, for independence only, was now impossible. Leading a rabble, Hidalgo and Allende were at first successful, but they had released forces beyond their control, they quarreled with each other, the Spanish Army regained control, and within a year the heads of Hidalgo, Allende, and two others were set up on the walls of the granary in Guanajuato, where they had scored their greatest triumph.

These men were not comparable to Washington, Adams, Jefferson, and the rest of our own Revolutionary leaders, but that was partly, I think, because the Spanish colonial government had been much more repressive than the English, and they and their followers had not acquired much political or military education. However, these were brave men who risked and lost their heads for their country, and in these towns on the night of September 15, 1810, was born the Republic of Mexico, which has suffered and achieved greatly and still has a long way to go, for the benefit of the whole human race.

On that night every year everyone packs into the *jardin* in San Miguel, which is specially lighted and is crowded also with several bands, drum and bugle corps, and detachments of militia and federal troops. At eleven o'clock, while fireworks explode everywhere, all the bands play different tunes, all the church bells ring deafeningly, and everyone tries to sing the national anthem, a track squad appears running down the hill on the main street, with every young man in it carrying a flaming torch. This symbolizes the arrival of the courier for Allende from the Corregidora of Querétaro. When the runners reach the front of the Presidencia, or City Hall, the Presidente steps forth an inch from the crowd on his narrow balcony, waves a Mexican flag, and shouts the Grito de Dolores. The words of this cry are quoted differently by different authorities, and I have never been able to *hear* one of them because of the tumult.

The next morning, there is a long parade of soldiers, bands, and school children, which ends when everyone stands massed in front of Allende's house on the *jardin* to listen to patriotic speeches. In a niche in the corner of the house there is a dead white statue of the hero, and over his door there is the proud inscription, *"Hic natus ubique notus."* The two leaders of the parade, mounted, are my barber impersonating Allende and some other man impersonating Father Hidalgo, with the banner of the Virgin of Guadalupe that they and the insurgent army picked up at the great shrine at Atotonilco on the way from Dolores to San Miguel.

Before being executed, Hidalgo was of course excommunicated, and the senior priest of San Miguel is naturally less prominent in these ceremonies than he is in that honoring Fray Juan de San Miguel, who founded the town. In the years since we first saw Independence Day celebrated in San Miguel in 1949, it seems to me that there has been a falling off of the popular enthusiasm. One night at the critical moment, in all the noise of bells, bands, and fireworks, I found myself shouting *"¡Viva México!"* almost alone. Don Carlos tells me that this impression is correct. He says that during the twenties on this night the *gachupínes,* still called that, remained in their houses, and he says that the change has been caused by increasing popular disgust with the one-party government of the PRI.

If less violently, Allende's birthday is celebrated in a similar manner, and one year the army sent a detachment of cavalry over from Querétaro. This kind of armed force may be slightly less obsolete in Mexico than elsewhere, and whether it is or not, the Mexicans are superb horsemen and put on a fine show. Early the next morning the detachment rode away, up our hill and out of town, with the sun gleaming on their helmets and their buglers playing a slow song of farewell — presumably to all the girls standing in the street who had been enchanted by the cavalrymen the night before. To our surprise, we found the whole spectacle as moving as it was medieval.

During these parades and celebrations, and whenever I visit the excellent historical museum in the castle of Chapultepec in the City, I find myself, as an American deeply sympathetic with the Mexican people and indebted to them, brooding at length on the history of this astonishing country, and on some of the political and economic questions it raises. I was about to say "the long, bloody history" of Mexico, but I am not sure that it has been any longer or any bloodier than any other. Disorganization, oppression, ignorance, banditry, and political assassination have been notable features of

this history, but Mexico, while indulging endlessly in civil
war, and while being invaded by Spain, the United States, and
France, has never invaded any other country or dropped a
bomb, atomic or otherwise, on any city. Disorganization has
a heavy price, still being paid here in many ways, but it
does weaken evil forces as well as good ones. The Germans
have a great talent for organization, and consider again what
they have done with it, to themselves and to the human race.
Since 1810 the Mexicans have wanted liberty first, whether
they know how to get it or not, and have continually risked
their lives for it. At 11:00 P.M., on every September 15, no
matter where I am, I am going to shout, *"¡Viva México!"*

On these patriotic occasions I always remember a story
told me by the late Dorsey Fisher about President Truman's
visit to Mexico. (Fisher, an exceptionally able Foreign
Service officer, was long the First Secretary of the American
Embassy in Mexico, and later held the same position in
Madrid. During the witch-hunt he was hounded from office,
and died soon afterwards.) About two o'clock one morning
President Truman, who had read much more history than
many American Presidents, called up President Alemán and
suggested that he would like, the next day, to place a wreath
on the monument to the "Boy Heroes" who died at Chapultepec Castle in the war with the United States in 1847. This
was arranged, of course, and Fisher said that of all the many

similar ceremonies he had seen in the course of his work
this was much the most moving and significant. There was
a vast crowd, and all the Mexican armed forces were represented. The American President's path to the base of the
monument was lined by tough Mexican generals, and not one
of their faces was dry. Fisher said that the effect went much
deeper than this emotionalism, and that, in his opinion,
nothing so good for Mexican-American relations had ever
been done by anyone.

I also think of this story whenever I have to go into the
Presidencia of San Miguel on some tax or water business.
On the staircase of that building there is a marble plaque
to two colonels from San Miguel who died in the war of
1847. The enemy in that war is unnamed on the plaque.
It so happens that my mother's father, then a young printer
from Ohio, also fought in that war. He later became a liberal
in politics, and so only patriotism, and perhaps a craving for
adventure, got him into that deplorable war. When my mother
wrote me that in his old age he had written a very short
autobiography, I was much pleased and interested, because
this boy, who was down here when Benito Juárez was a
young man, a century before I first came here, has become
to me almost a hallucinatory obsession, as one or another
of one's dead ancestors can do. However, the document was
very disappointing because it merely listed the barest facts
and dates of this youthful military adventure without comment. All my mother could add was that apparently this
boy conqueror was himself conquered by Mexico, because
long afterwards he was still talking about how much he
would like to return. Also, he took back to his mother in
Ohio a small fan that is one of the very few things in the
world that I should like someday to inherit. His name was
Charles N. Allen.

He died before I was born, but I was named for him and
for his son of the same name. Until I had to get a birth
certificate I thought that the Nicholas had been dropped

from my inheritance of the name. Whenever I cross the Rio Grande, coming south, the Mexican officials look at my birth certificate, assume that Allen was my father's surname and Smart my mother's, and then put me down on my Mexican papers as "Charles N. Allen S." Since official papers and lists tend to multiply themselves with the fecundity and the genetic precision of guinea pigs, I sometimes receive letters addressed in this manner. Sometimes I wonder whether, something like the hero of *Berkeley Square,* I shall one day awaken and find myself alive in Mexico in 1847 in the body and uniform of my grandfather. If, before I leave Mexico, a wreath is found one day beneath that plaque in the Presidencia of San Miguel de Allende, it will have been put there, in a sense, by Charles N. Allen.

33. *¡ADIÓS . . . !*

Despite what must seem like a lot of running around at night, to parties, cantinas, religious ceremonies, torchlight processions, fiestas, and so on, Peggy and I spend many more evenings quietly at home reading and then having a game of scrabble, which is a kind of sedative, before climbing up with Jamie through the moonlit patio to bed. On such evenings we sometimes think and talk about our life down here, and wonder how long we shall be here before we go home to stay. It is still chiefly a question of my work and of money, two matters in which we seem incapable of much foresight, and over which we seem to have little control. I might feel worse about being a drifter and a dilettante if I had not known many people of much greater resourcefulness, ambition, and self-confidence than my own whose lives have been shaped decisively, quite as much as mine, by forces beyond their prediction or control. In the Taoist Scriptures there are many shadowy hints about respecting these forces and finding one's way gently and irresistibly, like water. What we think we should like to do, if and when we can, is to live mostly at Oak Hill, but to come down here for several months each year to drink at these springs of inaction.

Going home every six months or year for a few weeks is not the same thing as going home to stay, because we are always rushed and we are always visiting, which can be after a while very tiring, however delightful. Still, these visits give us some idea of what that return will be.

My first responses are never very happy. The money problem rears its nasty head at once just on the other side of the Rio Grande, and it takes a conscious effort to stop translating dollars and cents back into pesos and allowing one's days to be shadowed by horrified thoughts of our expenses in terms of work and life in Mexico. Of course, all Americans look very white, and frankly not very handsome, but what is more troubling is the fact that so many of them look as though they were enjoying life very little indeed, and had not enjoyed it for a long time. Most of them seem to be incredibly free, rich, and comfortable, but a lot of good it seems to do them. Too many of the older people seem to have nothing to feel or think about, too many of the middle-aged and young married people seem to be almost frantic about the complexities of their lives, too many of the young people seem to be conservatives, and unwilling and unhappy fatalists, too many of the children seem to be quarreling, neurotic little wrecks and savages, and too many of the men of all ages seem to have almost invisible rings in their noses, with their women holding the chains. Many exceptions appear, and these dismal impressions fade in time, but never entirely.

Then there is the ugliness. The roadside signs have almost obliterated landscapes that on the whole must have been richer, subtler, and even more various than those of Mexico, if usually less spectacular. And if you look at these signs you get a picture of an Ideal Life, offered to the consumers with success, that I find a Hell more terrible in its sterility and monotony than that imagined by Hieronymus Bosch. Then, as the signs, the used car lots, the abandoned car dumps, and the roadside night clubs thicken, we come into the cities and towns, most of which seem to me ugly and depressing beyond any question and without any excuse. Slums are bad, and similar, everywhere, but even the better suburbs, with their lawns and gardens, seem to me wasteful, smug, and very dull. After three or four days of driving north, I am almost at the point of saying to myself, "Well, if you don't like it here in the United States why don't you go back where you came from?"

But before I reach that low point, we are driving up through Kentucky, which is good, and then at last we cross the Ohio River, which I consider one of the noblest in the world that I have seen. Every time we cross it or drive along beside it, it looks almost as good to me as it did when I went down it aboard an LST, conceivably looking at my native land for the last time. Then we are in Ohio, which is home. Texas, Virginia, Vermont, and some other states make much more noise about themselves, but Ohio suits me very well, thank you. The people may be as hagridden as elsewhere, but I think I see in their eyes, often enough, a quiet, humorous, and skeptical serenity. The towns may be as ugly as elsewhere, but to me they look as though they had been made and were lived in by people who see them now and again, and enjoy them. Stopping in a restaurant or drugstore, I can understand every word I hear and, more important, I know, more or less, what these people are thinking and feeling, and what made them that way. When I see a farmer backing a tractor out of a barn, with his dog barking gleefully, and driving it down into a cornfield, I could write a much better story about him and his family, his politics, his religion, his worries and his satisfactions, than I ever could about a rich *ranchero* in Mexico, or about an Indian in white behind his wooden plow. I am not going to write stories about either, but this capacity, which is not limited to storytellers, is important to my particular sense of being alive in depth.

Finally we come into Chillicothe, Ohio, a town that in beauty may not be much above the average of those on the way up from the Rio Grande: I couldn't say. It merely happens to be the town whose quiet, subtle beauties of old "mansion" or shanty, of back yard and riverbank, have grown on and fed me for many years. Here, since I was a small boy sent down from Cleveland on vacation, or always returning from New York, or New England, or Europe, finally with a bride, I have worked and idled, loved and laughed, played the fool and suffered, all more deeply than anywhere else in the world. More important to me than the town is the countryside, whose ranges of blue hills, hidden little valleys and villages, and broad river bottoms all change so beautifully and so subtly through the year. That countryside is in my blood, and there is nothing remotely resembling it in Mexico.

We go to visit old friends now, and we love ours as much as you do yours, but the most intense moment comes the day after our arrival. After calling up our tenants, in whom we are incredibly lucky, we take Jamie into the car, drive out the Cincinnati pike and up the hill, clank across the outer cattle guard into our front pasture, and drive very slowly past the pine plantation and under the great old tulip trees and the last few ancient oaks towards the big old stone house with the vines and the solid wood shutters that is Oak Hill and home. For both of us this gracious and dignified, shabby and difficult old place is rich with memories of delight and pain, yet it is as calming and peaceful as it is exciting. The spirits of all the good people who lived there before us seem to greet us with calm good cheer and reassurance every time we enter that yard, that ancient garden, and that big, cool, shadowy hall that goes all the way through the house to the sunlight again, with the familiar and beloved shapes of the blue Huntington hills beyond. Then we wander through the high-ceilinged old rooms looking at pictures, sitting in chairs, picking up books, looking out of this tall window and that, remembering so much and hoping for more. Making its own demands, which are not slight but have never been just too much, this old place has fed our bodies, minds, and spirits for many years. With luck, and despite my erratic character and fortunes, we shall live there again, at length, in the old ways always a little new and fresh, and die there at the same time, laughing.

However, we know very well that when there comes that time of true return, despite all the deep satisfactions of life at Oak Hill, there will be plenty of times when we shall think happily and even longingly of Mexico, of San Miguel, and of our little house here. Since the time of my great-grandfather — who built Oak Hill, and who, judging from his daguerreotype, probably had plenty of troubles of his own — none of us has ever lived there without anxiety about money and without the unending grind of housework. ("Maria . . . !") There something is always rotting away or breaking down or becoming overgrown, and we haven't been able to

afford a man for fifteen years. ("Cipriano ... !") When we tramp through the February slush and sleet on Paint Street we shall remember the balmy, bright winter mornings in the *jardin* and out in the vast desert, with the ducks circling above the water. How often then shall we remember all these good people without ambition or fear; the hours of totally free and happy work and the drowsy siestas; the days on the great beaches and in the distant mountains; the unhurried rambles in the streets and park with a good dog; the enchanted struggle with art; the long, happy talks with friends who were not too busy or tired for living; the guitars with the falling voices, the chanting in the churches, and the band music before the first bull bursts into the plaza; the children playing games in our little street and asking for magazines; the old woman with her one egg, and Carlitos with his puppy; all this and so much more, and over the ancient pink little town the vast sky changing towards evening, the blackbirds flying down to roost in the *jardin,* and the church bells ringing.

¡Adiós! ¡Adiós ... !

NOTE ON MONEY, PAPERS, AND BOOKS

We have received so many inquiries about the costs and legal difficulties of living in Mexico that a few words on these subjects may be in order.

The dollar is now worth 12.50 pesos, and we get 12.47 at our bank, which makes the peso worth eight cents. In 1954 the peso was devalued from 8.60; the prices of American goods rose at once, and other prices have since risen almost equivalently. At the present time the peso seems fairly secure, in relation to the dollar, and inflation slow but steady.

My wife and I seem to live here, in the style here described, on about two hundred dollars a month. Some single Americans and couples seem to live on much less; others on much more. In Mexico City and the tourist places the costs are much higher, and in remote villages, if you can rough it, they are lower. We figure that in general, in terms of dollars, costs are about one third of those in the States. Some things, such as refrigerators and matches, cost more here than in the States; others, such as liquor and cigarettes, cost less than a third as much. A car is very useful for seeing the country, and for two or more people with luggage it provides the cheapest way to travel to and from the States, but a car is by no means indispensable. For our house we had been paying about twenty dollars U.S. a month in rent, almost unfurnished, and had spent two or three hundred dollars on furniture. We bought it for thirty-two hundred dollars, and then spent about eight hundred dollars more on necessary improvements. We now rent the place, when we do rent it, pretty well furnished, with utilities, maid, and part-time gardener, for seventy-five dollars a month. Decent places can be rented cheaper, and handsome establishments for twice as much. It should be remembered that none of these figures includes trips to the States, car accidents, or hospitalization in Mexico City. We always try to keep a few hundred dollars in handy reserve.

At the present time we are here on tourist cards, which are good for 180 days only. Before the end of that time we have to leave the country for twenty-four hours, with our car and with any electrical gadgets, typewriters, etc., that we have imported. These are listed on the car permit. Once a year it is permitted to impound the car and these things at the customs house in Mexico City, fly out of the country and back, and then secure an extension of the car permit. All of this represents a considerable nuisance and expense, but persons holding student's papers, for example, although allowed to remain a year, are limited in the amount of time they can remain out of Mexico without losing their papers, and when we have returned to the States, lectures, an operation, and other matters have twice kept us longer than we had anticipated. It is possible to deposit several thousand dollars (the figure changes) with the Mexican Government, receive this back in monthly and certain installments, without interest, over a period of years, and receive at once greater freedom of movement and action as an *inmigrado*. It is also possible to be admitted for six months as a *visitante,* with permission to buy property within that time. On tourist papers it is not necessary to have a passport, but we got ours in order to fly once to Guatemala, and shall keep it renewed. Births and deaths provide additional complications. For further and more precise and up-to-date information on all these matters it is advisable to consult a Mexican consul in the United States or a good English-speaking lawyer in Mexico City. When the restrictions seem difficult and expensive, and when the officials seem inconsistent or ill informed, it is to be remembered that this is true for less privileged aliens in the United States and in most countries in the world. The Comisión Nacional de Turismo, Avenida Juárez 76, México, D.F., can be very helpful in pinches or in general.

As relative beginners, we have found the following books the most interesting and useful: *True History of the Conquest of New Spain,* by Bernal Díaz del Castillo, 1581; *Life in Mexico during a Residence of Two Years in that Country,* by Mme. Calderón de la Barca, 1843; *Viva Mexico!* by Charles Macomb Flandrau, 1908; *A Treasury of Mexican Folkways,* by Frances Toor, 1947; *The United States and Mexico,* by Howard F. Cline, 1953; *A History of Mexico,* by Henry Bamford Parkes, 1950; and *Investment in Mexico,* by the U.S. Department of Commerce, 1955.